Working in the Catholic Church

An Attitudinal Survey by the National Association of Church Personnel Administrators

Sheed & Ward

Sheed & Ward™ is a service of The National Catholic Reporter Publishing Company.

Library of Congress Cataloguing-in-Publication Data

Working in the Catholic Church : NACPA attitudinal survey.
     p.   cm.
   ISBN 1-55612-568-2 (alk. paper)
    1. Catholic Church--United States--Employees--Attitudes. I. National Association of Church Personnel Administrators (U.S.)
BX1407.E45W67 1993
331.2'04128273--dc20   93-19042
                                        CIP

Published by: Sheed & Ward
                   115 E. Armour Blvd. P.O. Box 419492
                   Kansas City, MO 64141-6492

To order, call: (800) 333-7373

Cover design by John Murello

13.31

4-20-94

Contents

Introduction

JOB SATISFACTION IN THE CHURCH WORK PLACE

What is it like to work for Catholic Church administrative offices, parishes, institutions? How do the priests, lay persons, and members of religious communities view the Catholic Church as an employer? How do they view their working conditions? How do the laity in general feel about their family members working for the Catholic Church?

To address these questions, the National Association of Church Personnel Administrators (NACPA) conducted a national survey of persons who work in Catholic Church settings. The survey assessed the job satisfaction of those employees: priests, lay persons, and religious. At a time of major transitions in the Catholic Church in general and in the composition of church workers/ministers in particular, the survey explored the church environment as a place of employment.

Two major changes have been taking place in the church workforce in the post-Vatican II era. It is both a time of ever-expanding involvement of lay persons in their rightful place as ministers and also a time of rapidly decreasing numbers of ordained and vowed persons working long-term in church settings. These trends make it critical to assess the attitudes of all church workers in order to make projections for church employment needs of the future. During this time of transition, it is important to identify mutual expectations and make conscious choices in building the church workforce for the next century. What are the compelling issues that need to be addressed in order for the church to continue to carry forward its mission through the persons it employs?

The primary assumption which church leaders traditionally have held about church work is that the church setting provides a great deal of job satisfaction. The Catholic bishops' pastoral on the United States economy, "Economic Justice for All," espouses these values. However, whether these values are operative in church settings has not been verified by any research on a national scale although the assumption continues to be a context out of which many church employees operate.

Specific dimensions of job satisfaction were addressed in the survey from the perspectives of both the church administrators who employ church workers and all workers as employees.

Areas of importance in assessing job satisfaction from the perspective of those who employ and supervise church workers include

1. recruitment and retention of competent employees
2. defined and published personnel policies
3. affirmative action policies
4. recruitment and placement practices
5. attitudes toward church workers

From the perspective of the employee, the following areas are important:

1. participation in decision making
2. pay and benefits
3. training and development
4. just treatment of legitimate grievances,
5. supervision, performance appraisal, recognition
6. opportunities for advancement and promotion
7. job security

The survey assessed both church employees and employees on the aspects of

1. satisfaction with responsibilities and involvement in ministry
2. enrichment through church environment
3. desire for long-term church employment
4. equal expectations for lay, religious, priests
5. influence of satisfaction with church practices in general on level of satisfaction with church

The results of the survey provide direction for future NACPA services to human resource managers in the Catholic Church. The National Association of Church Personnel Administrators will continue to develop services to support ways in which the church provides a positive employment relationship and to improve conditions or attitudes for optimal job satisfaction for church workers.

CHURCH PERSONNEL ADMINISTRATION

NACPA is the only national organization whose primary focus is just treatment for those persons who work for the church: priests, lay persons, and religious. It serves women and men who are charged with the human resource management in the Catholic Church throughout the United States. Its mission is to identify skills and competencies for human resource managers; to develop personnel systems which integrate management and pastoral values; and to advocate standards of just treatment for church personnel.

NACPA has grown to over 1,200 members in its 20 year history. Its members today include an equal number of women and men who serve in the church as diocesan priests, permanent deacons, lay women and men, and women and men religious. These persons serve in diocesan central offices, congregations of religious, parishes, church-related organizations, and agencies.

The survey of attitudes of employees of the church grows out of NACPA's primary focus in recent years for advocacy for just treatment for church employees. A premiere publication which states NACPA's just treatment philosophy is the document, "Just Treatment for Those Who Work for the Church." It was released in November 1986 at the same time that the National Council of Catholic Bishops completed the second draft of the economics pastoral, "Economic Justice for All." The NACPA document is a manual for the implementation of the pastoral within the internal structures of the church, and NACPA services provide education and assistance with that implementation. The document offers ethical principles, specific statements on personnel policy areas, and advocates a comprehensive approach to church personnel administration.

Since that time, NACPA has offered just treatment seminars in several regions of the country for implementation within dioceses, religious congregations, church-related organizations, and parishes. It also offers consultant services in assessing and developing personnel systems in these same settings. Other publications provide hands-on manuals for administrators in areas of policy development, performance appraisal, parish personnel administration, and compensation administration.

To expand the implementation of the Just Treatment document, NACPA convened a meeting of other national church organizations in April 1987. The leadership of these national organizations endorsed the document and pledged to work for its implementation within their own sphere of influence. They continue to meet annually to forward these concerns.

CHURCH WORK PLACE ISSUES

Perhaps more than any other church or international organization in recent history, the Catholic Church has undergone dramatic and far-reaching changes in the 25 years since the Second Vatican Council. It continues to be an institution in transition, and one of the most apparent changes is the rapid shift in persons working as full-time administrators, ministers and support staff charged with carrying forward the mission of the Catholic Church in the United States.

The changes in NACPA's membership during its 20-year history reflect this rapid shift. Begun in 1971 from one service area of the National Federal of Priests Councils, the new organization expanded its membership to men and women religious. Today it numbers over 1,200 persons with 37% diocesan priests, 40% religious, and 23% lay persons.

Several context issues emerged during these periods of rapid change. One issue concerns expectations for church work—differing and perhaps unrealistic or conflicting expectations both on the part of the Catholic laity in general and also on the part of persons providing this work. There are sometimes differing expectations between and among the different groups of workers—priests/religious/lay, administrators/employees, exempt/non-exempt employees and those in diocesan offices/parishes/religious congregations.

There certainly are different and differing theologies, ecclesiologies and experiences of church among persons in the church work place and also among those being served. People also have varying interpretations and levels of acceptance of church regulations. All of these context issues impact attitudes concerning job satisfaction among church workers. The ambiguity, contradictions, and misperceptions resulting from these different perspectives are contained within the findings of the survey of church workers. Therefore, the findings need to be interpreted within all of these broader contexts as well as the more specific context areas.

DESCRIPTION OF THE STUDY

Study Design

NACPA contracted with the Gallup Organization to conduct the survey to determine how the employees and Catholic laity in general viewed working conditions in Catholic Church settings.

Two focus groups were conducted with church administrators and employees in the Archdiocese of Indianapolis. Separate sessions were conducted with priests and with employees representing religious, lay ministers, deacons, and lay employees. Participants were carefully chosen to be representative of the various functions that would later be sampled in the final studies; e.g., diocesan and parish office administrators and employees, educators, social workers, inner-city employees.

These sessions provided an understanding of the potential concerns, issues, tensions, needs and challenges confronting church administrators and employees. The results aided in the preparation of the questionnaire drafts which were developed by Gallup and reviewed by NACPA. Following revisions requested by the NACPA staff and Task Force, the employee and administrator questionnaire drafts were pretested in the following locations:

Diocese of Rochester, New York
Diocese of Grand Rapids, Michigan
Diocese of Galveston-Houston, Texas
Diocese of Salt Lake City, Utah

The four dioceses were selected for the pilot study to be representative of the diverse composition of the church according to both geographical and employment conditions. A NACPA member was contacted in each of the dioceses and asked to distribute questionnaires to representative administrators and employees in nonsupervisory positions. Careful instructions were given so that the questionnaires would reflect a diverse pool of respondents, both according to function and to attitudinal predisposition. It would have defeated the purpose of the study to obtain views from only those who are known to maintain a highly positive attitude towards their employment with the church.

In the pretest, questionnaires were sent to 80 employees and to 20 administrators. Questionnaires were returned by 69 employees and 18 administrators. Review by Gallup and by NACPA representatives led to the conclusion that the draft questionnaires would meet the survey objectives, provided minor adjustments suggested by the pretest results were made. The final questionnaire differed from the pilot questionnaires only in minor respects, and it was decided to include the pilot questionnaires in the final tabulating base so that the dioceses they represent would not be omitted from the study.

A parallel questionnaire was developed for members of the Catholic laity to gain an understanding of their perceptions and opinions of working conditions with the church. Question wording was adjusted as necessary to reflect the perspective of the laity.

Phases of the Study

The final study consisted of three phases:

1. The *first phase* surveyed administrators with supervisory responsibilities. Questionnaires were mailed to 925 administrators who are members of NACPA. This included persons serving in diocesan central offices and parishes from 165 dioceses as well as numerous congregations of women and men religious. The questionnaire was also sent to 373 administrators from 61 dioceses not represented in the NACPA membership. There was a 52% response rate with 692 persons returning the administrator survey.

The demographic characteristics of the administrators who participated in the survey are: 25% priests, 46% religious, and 29% lay employees; 53% male and 47% female . Of the total respondents 51% were over 50 years of age and 94% of them had at least an undergraduate college degree while 84% had post college graduate education. The employers for the administrators in the survey were: 10% parishes, 56% diocesan offices, 29% religious congregation mother-houses. The administrators live in the following regions of the country: 23% East, 45% Midwest, 15% South, and 15% West.

2. The *second phase* of the study surveyed employees which included professional and support staff. Questionnaires were mailed to 1,340 employees; 669 or 50% responded.

Administrators in 40 dioceses were asked to provide lists of employees in their dioceses. These dioceses were chosen to represent varying sizes, ethnic populations, and regions of the country. Participant lists were provided from the following types of dioceses: 10 large dioceses, 11 medium sized dioceses, and 6 small dioceses.

Administrators from 20 different religious congregations from varying regions of the country were contacted for lists of employees at their motherhouses. Nine contact persons provided lists of employees for the survey.

These employees were chosen according to instructions provided by Gallup. The places of employment included: diocesan central offices, parish pastoral offices and schools, religious congregation motherhouses. The contact persons were asked to supply the names and addresses of employees in the full range of positions: middle managers, pastors, business managers, principals of schools, secretaries, maintenance staff, pastoral associates, teachers, cooks, liturgists, youth ministers.

Demographic characteristics of the employees included: 14% priests, 21% religious, and 65% lay employees; 43% male and 57% female. About 36% of the respondents were over 50 years of age, and 75% had an undergraduate college degree and 56% had post college graduate education. The employers for the employees in the survey were: 37% parish, 51% diocesan offices, and 9% religious congregation motherhouses. The employees live in the following regions of the country: 20% East, 57% Midwest, 9% South, and 14% West.

3. In the *third phase,* telephone interviews were conducted with a nationwide sample of 500 Catholics, ages 18 and older.

Mailing Procedures

All mail questionnaires were sent from Gallup's Princeton office. The mailings, enclosed in an outer Gallup envelope, were similar to those used in the pilot study; i.e., cover letter from Gallup, the questionnaire, and a prepaid return envelope to Gallup.

Telephone Interviewing Procedures

All telephone interviews were conducted from Gallup's central telephone interviewing facilities in Houston, Texas. The interviewers received special instructions on the survey and were continuously supervised and monitored to ensure correct application of the sampling and questioning methodologies.

A nationwide sample of adults was contacted for the survey and screened so that only those who identified themselves as Catholics were interviewed. The obtained sample was compared with the known statistical characteristics of Catholics, as measured by a continuous monitor of religious preferences on Gallup surveys, and results were weighted to adjust for sample imbalances so that the tabulations would be representative of all Catholics in the U.S.

Tabulations and Report

All questionnaires were received directly by Gallup, were prepared for data entry, entered, verified, and tabulated independently by Gallup. The report was prepared independently by Gallup.

ANALYSIS OF THE SURVEY RESULTS

The survey results point to areas of significant satisfaction in the church work place and to specific concerns about job satisfaction for persons who work for Catholic Church institutions. In order to gain the maximum information and implications of the data, NACPA engaged a sociologist and church personnel administrators to analyze and expand the results of the survey.

Sociological Analysis

All of the data was analyzed by a sociologist who provided a review of literature, analysis of the findings of the survey, relationships with other appropriate data, and offered discussion and conclusions on the topic areas. This analysis is found in the five chapters of Part I.

Church Personnel Administrators' Analysis and Expansion of Topics

Six church personnel administrators were engaged to continue the analysis of the findings and to expand the discussion of the issues indicating implications and suggesting responses. This analysis was developed in the following topic areas of the survey:

1. Training and Development
2. Recruitment, Retention, Job Descriptions, Performance Appraisal
3. Grievance Procedures
4. Compensation: Pay and Benefits
5. Affirmative Action

Chapter 6 contains the analysis of the topic area, "Training and Development." The author explores church workers' interest in further education and sabbaticals and their rating of education benefits. She also explores the issue of promotion, interest and importance for various groups, actual opportunities, the relationship to consideration of employment elsewhere, the ability to retain competent employees, and the need for future preparation of employees. How Catholics in general value continuing education for church workers is also reported.

Chapter 7 covers "Recruitment, Retention, Job Descriptions, and Performance Appraisal." The issue of hiring and retaining competent employees is explored in this chapter with specific focus on recruitment, job clarity, and the presence or frequency of performance appraisal. How these aspects of the employment relationship are present and implemented for the various groups of church workers is reported and compared. The author also discusses these issues in the context of the employees' desire always to work for the church.

Chapter 8 addresses the final topic area of the survey, "Grievance Procedures." The focus of the chapter is the expectation by church workers of being treated justly by the church employer in the instance of legitimate grievances. This issue is explored for differences and similarities between and among various groups of workers. The authors also address the issue in relation to job clarity, performance appraisal, perceptions of job security, open discussion of work difficulties with supervisors, and participation in decision making within the church work place. The chapter is set in the context of "due process" principles and the presence of specific procedures.

Chapter 9 addresses church workers' perceptions of "Compensation." It explores the adequacy of church workers' pay and benefits both for meeting their own needs and the needs of their families or religious congregations. The chapter also includes such issues as willingness of employees to sacrifice in order to work for the church, the extent to which that is possible, and whether workers are considering employment elsewhere because of compensation. The attitudes toward the ability to hire and retain competent employees, present job security, and future retirement security are also reported. The perceptions on these issues of Catholics not working for the church are also included.

The exploration of the church workers' attitudes on "Affirmative Action" are covered in Chapter 10. The author explores the perceptions of the church's record in hiring and promoting women and minorities. He compares the responses of women and men and persons of different age groups around this and related issues. Perceptions of Affirmative Action in general and with specific groups are addressed. The author compares these perceptions with actual data from other studies within the church setting.

Reflections in Part II indicate directions in responding to the results of the attitudinal survey and future use of the survey and its data.

ACKNOWLEDGEMENTS

Many persons contributed to the successful completion of this project of the National Association of Church Personnel Administrators. We are grateful to the National Board of NACPA for its initiation of the project and support during its implementation and to the Board Task Force who assisted in the preparation of the survey materials and review of the findings: Mrs. Mary Kessler, Rev. J. Patrick Murphy, CM, Mr. Thomas Schroeder, and Sr. Barbara Thiella, SND.

Special appreciation is due to Sister Loretta Schafer, SP, Chancellor of the Archdiocese of Indianapolis, who gathered focus groups for the development of the questionnaires and to those who participated in these groups. We appreciate the assistance of the contact persons in piloting the questionnaires in their dioceses. The survey would have been impossible without the assistance of the NACPA members and other diocesan administrators and religious congregation leaders who provided names for the participant lists of employees. And of course, persons who responded to the questions, both the written survey and the telephone interview, provided important data.

We are grateful to the sociologist and church personnel administrators who provided the analysis and development of the material found in Chapters 6 through 10.

The Gallup Organization, Inc. conducted the survey of NAPCA, and we appreciate the continued consultation services of the project coordinator, Robert Bezilla.

As the task of responding to the results of the survey takes shape, NACPA has called together church administrators to assist with their expertise in planning programs and services in response to the results of the survey. The following participated in a three-day planning session: Sr. Judian Breitenback, PHJC, Most Rev. Gerald Gettelfinger, Rev. Jeffrey Godecker, Mrs. Patricia Gries, Ms. Mary Ellen McClanaghan, Mr. Thomas Meehan, and Sr. Lorraine Villemaire, SSJ.

The analysis of the survey as well as the publication and distribution of the findings were funded by a grant from the Lilly Endowment, Indianapolis, Indiana. We are grateful for the assistance of Sr. Jeanne Knorle, SP, in the administration of the grant.

Part I

Sociological Analysis

— 1 —

Training, Development and Promotion
by Patricia Wittberg, S.C.

The first topic area to be considered in analyzing the NACPA survey results will deal with the opportunities for training and development which are possessed by workers in Catholic Church related positions. The results are reported in two groups: administrators, (persons with supervisory responsibilities); and employees, (professional and support staff). The general format of this section will also be followed in subsequent sections: first, an overview will be presented of the sociological and business literature concerning education and employee development for all types of organizations. Following this section on overall theory and research will be a more specific review of the literature on the ongoing training and development of priests, religious and laity in church employment. The third section will summarize the findings of the NACPA survey, and a final discussion will link these findings to the studies reviewed in the first two sections. For Topic Area A, this pattern will be repeated a second time to cover the separate issue of promotion.

TRAINING AND DEVELOPMENT

THEORETICAL BACKGROUND

The Human Relations School

An extensive and wide-ranging literature in sociology, psychology and business management covers the need to provide training and development for employees. The most well-known school of research and writing on this topic is the Human Relations School, in which several hundred studies have been done since the 1930's. The basic assumption of the Human Relations theorists is that organizations with satisfied and motivated workers will be more productive. The primary task of management, therefore, is to foster this satisfaction and motivation among employees. One way of doing so was outlined by Frederick Herzberg (1966, 1982), who held that employees have two basically different sets of needs. The first, which Herzberg called "job hygiene" or "maintenance" needs, related principally to safety and comfort in the workplace. The second category of needs, which is more relevant to the topic of this paper, are the "job enrichment" needs:

> The principles of job enrichment require that the job be developed to include new aspects which provide the opportunity for the employee's psychological growth . . . Merely to add one undemanding job to another or to switch from one undemanding job to another is not adequate . . . Job enrichment calls for . . . opportunities for achievement, responsibility, recognition, growth and learning. (Pugh and Hickson, 1989:201-2)

Following Herzberg's theories, a number of writers in business and management have emphasized the opportunity for employees to expand their knowledge and skills on the job. The Hay Group's report, for example, noted that "challenge" and "new skills" were top-ranked work values among managers and professionals (Hay Group, p.III-3). However, many jobs do not fulfill these values: 71% of the managers and 53% of the professionals in the Hay study felt that their work was challenging and interesting, whereas only 31% of the clerical workers did. Also, 67% of the managers and 53% of the professionals rated their places of work favorably with regard to providing opportunities to develop new skills and talents, while fewer than 40% of the clerical workers did so. (Hay Group, p.III-12). Women were more likely to value the opportunity to learn new skills than men were (Hay Group, p.III-4). Fewer than half of the employees in all categories said that their companies trained them well. (Hay Group, p.IV-20)

Human Relations theorists, therefore, focus on the need for organizations to foster satisfaction and motivation in their employees. Opportunities for on-the-job training, continuing education, personal development and sabbaticals are considered to be essential determinants of worker satisfaction. Several sociologists, however, have criticized Human Relations theory. As early as 1967, research by House and Wigdor found that the causes of job satisfaction varied widely from individual to individual. Subsequent studies by Fein (1976) found little support for either the accuracy of Human Relations research or the relevance of the individual cases it studied to other real-life situations. By the mid-1980's, both sociologists (Perrow, 1986:86,114-119) and psychologists (Neff, 1985:140-41) were warning their readers that surprisingly little empirical evidence existed for better performance among more satisfied employees:

In considering this entire approach to the psychology of work, two observations are in order. First, despite more than two decades of intensive effort, the precise nature of the relationship between work satisfaction and work efficiency remains elusive. Second, *satisfaction* is too abstract a term to tell us very much about the affect sides of work. (Neff, 1985:140)

If the basic assumption of a link between employee satisfaction and productivity is thus called into question, the derived corollary of a link between job enrichment programs, satisfaction and productivity will also become less certain. Recently, one study has even found a *negative* relationship between company provided opportunities for on-going training and a firm's productivity. (Kelly and Harrison, 1990) Such programs, these authors felt, were most common in the largest organizations, whose employees might be more generally alienated than the employees of smaller businesses, even if the smaller businesses provided fewer formal training opportunities. The effect of organization size, in other words, overrode the effect of ongoing training and sabbaticals.

The Labor Process School and the Deskilling of Labor

Why, then, do the majority of writers and researchers continue to ascribe to the Human Relations School, if so little evidence exists to support their claims? Perrow argues (1986:49-52) that the basic function of such writing is ideological. Throughout the twentieth century, a process of "deskilling" has been occurring, whereby the tasks of factory workers (Braverman, 1974), office staffs (Glenn and Feldberg, 1977), and even engineers and other professionals (Shaiken, 1986; Garson, 1988) are broken down into smaller, compartmentalized bits which can each be learned by a different, less-skilled employee. This deskilling deprives the employee of opportunities to learn or to exercise personal discretion on the job. Employers can also fire expensive and assertive skilled workers and substitute cheaper and more docile ones, who are frequently minorities or women. Several authors (e.g. Crozier, 1964; Pfeiffer, 1980) have even noted deliberate management efforts to keep lower-level employees from acquiring the kind of knowledge which would empower them in their dealings with the organization. The restructuring of the workplace implied by deskilling also enables firms to increase in size. Kelly and Harrison (1990) speculate that this size increase is the reason, along with the power advantages that deskilling confers on management, why organizational initiatives toward increasing employee training or participation do not result in greater productivity or satisfaction. Many of the companies which initiate such programs are so large and impersonal that their efforts lead to little real change in the workers' job conditions.

Inherent in the deskilling process is a basic contradiction between the need to motivate workers and the need to produce the organization's product or service efficiently. Confined to one repetitive job, workers become bored and alienated. They no longer have the knowledge or the authority to respond creatively in unusual situations, and management may be too far removed to notice that change is needed. The organization may thus become locked in to the status quo, and its various component groups may be involved primarily in protecting their own interests. Sporadic efforts may be made to combat this tendency by imitating (e.g.) Japanese or Swedish models of worker involvement (See Ouchi, 1982), but these usually fall short of any real change. In the long run, the deskilling of labor at all levels results in an inability to cope with change and a lack of competitiveness vis-a-vis foreign companies. (Shaiken, 1986) Another complication, as a recent U.S. Department of Labor study pointed out, is that the workforce will grow much more slowly in the 1990's than it did in previous decades. This will result in increased competition by business for qualified employees. (Bolick and Nestleroth, 1988:34) In a tighter hiring market, firms which have deskilled their jobs may have difficulty attracting and retaining workers.

RESEARCH ON CHURCH WORKERS AND EDUCATION

Priests

Several studies have been done during the past two decades of the opportunities available to priests for training and development, and both the old and the new studies are in substantial agreement with the Human Relations Theory in stressing the importance of continuing education for clergy satisfaction. Hall and Schneider (1973), writing in the Human Relations tradition, held that priests' self-esteem was increased through working toward a challenging goal. Without challenges, they became dependent and passive. A more recent study by Scheets (1989a:6) supported Hall's and Schneider's findings that priests' satisfaction and self-perceived competence was increased by education. Scheets (1989a:7) also found that younger priests were more likely than older ones to favor sabbaticals (77% to 46%) and other opportunities for professional advancement (58% to 30%).

According to the National Organization for Continuing Education of Roman Catholic Clergy (1986:1-10), the institutional church has stressed the importance of continuing education for its priests in a wide range of official documents and has set up guidelines for yearly retreats, regular workshops and study days, and possible opportunities for graduate study or sabbaticals. To achieve these goals, church officials have provided educational benefits that are roughly comparable with those received by ministers in mainline Protestant churches. According to Hoge, Carroll and Scheets (1988:51), Catholic priests across the country received an average of $531 in educational allowances in 1986, as compared to the amounts received by Episcopalian priests ($598), Lutheran ministers ($544) and Methodist ministers ($473).

Researchers have disagreed on how much priests avail themselves of their educational opportunities. A study of priests in the Joliet diocese by Fogarty (1988:73) found that 36.4% of the priests there ranked continuing education "very important" and 41.2% "important," but that fewer said they availed themselves of continuing education opportunities "very frequently" (13.4%) or "frequently" (40.9%). Scheets' study (1989a) of clergy in Elizabeth, NJ, found that over 80% agreed they needed more education in contrast to 58% of the New England clergy he had studied (Scheets 1989b:10). This contrasts with earlier research by Ference (1971:510) and Kantowicz (1983:2), who noted a strain of anti-intellectualism among the Washington and Chicago priests they studied, which seemed to be based upon the idea that intellectual pursuits encouraged individualism and attenuated a team spirit.

Women Religious and Lay Church Workers

Fewer studies have been done of educational opportunities for women religious, and still fewer on lay workers, male religious and deacons. According to Hoge, Carroll and Scheets (1988:56), sisters received $419 for educational expenses in comparison to the priests' $531. Only 64% of lay workers received any educational allowance at all. Among those who did, the allowance averaged $495. By and large, as one study found (Rosenberg and Sullivan 1980:76), women religious working in parish ministry were more highly educated than the laywomen in parish ministry: 60% of the sisters had some graduate or professional school credits and an additional 29% had their bachelor's. In contrast, only 15% of the total sample of parish workers had their bachelors and 11% had graduate training. 50% of Rosenberg's and Sullivan's total sample of parish ministers had no training at all. The figures on sisters' greater than average education are supported by Neal's work (1984:31). With regard to opportunities for future training, of the 440 women religious in new ministries interviewed by Joseph (1982:93), 50% had congregationally supplied opportunities for sabbaticals and 45% for summer educational leave. 34% rated the availability of congregational funding for professional development as adequate, 20% as inadequate, and 28% gave no response.

Especially in situations such as the Catholic Church, where opportunities for advancement to decision-making levels are often limited to ordained priests, education and training are important as alternate sources of authority. La Magdeleine (1986:323) points out that a potential for conflict exists when the priests in a parish or diocese attempt to make decisions on the basis of their position in an articulated chain of command (so-called "line positions") and the religious or lay workers argue that *they* should be the ones to decide policy because of their greater or more specialized training. This conflict can lead to dissatisfaction and more rapid job turnover among religious and lay employees. (Wittberg, 1989b; Fox, 1986)

FINDINGS OF THE CURRENT STUDY

Q.12a and Q.12c: Opportunity for Sabbaticals and Other Educational Opportunities

Within the analysis of the study the term sabbatical is defined broadly as time away from full-time work for personal or professional enrichment or education. Overall, a larger percentage of administrators (73.9%) than of employees (65.5%) considered the opportunity for sabbaticals to be "important" or "very important." Among administrators, women valued sabbaticals more than men; the reverse was true among employees. (This finding replicates that of the Hay Group noted above.) Sabbaticals were more important for respondents with college or graduate degrees, but this difference, while still statistically significant,[1] was less pronounced among the employee respondents than among the administrators. As Scheets (1989a) had discovered in his study of younger priests, the employees and administrators in this study who were under 50 years old valued sabbaticals more than those over 50. Longtime administrators and employees, however, were more likely to value sabbaticals than recently-hired ones. Among administrators, those working for religious congregations were the most interested in sabbaticals; among employees this category ranked least.

An equally high percentage of priests, women religious and men religious, both administrators and employees, ranked sabbaticals as important. Lay respondents and deacons ranked lower (although over half of these latter categories were interested in sabbaticals).

Employees in charities, parishes and diocesan central offices were less likely (60-66%) than those in education, health and youth ministries (74-78%) to say that sabbaticals were important. Administrators in education, youth work and parishes were more likely (80-100%) to rank sabbaticals as important than were administrators in the other fields, but

---

1. The word "significant" has a specific meaning in statistical research. Whenever the term is used in these reports, it will mean that it is at least 95% certain that the relationship being described really does exist, among all the employees and administrators who work for the church.

Table 1
% Saying Sabbaticals "Very" or "Fairly" Important

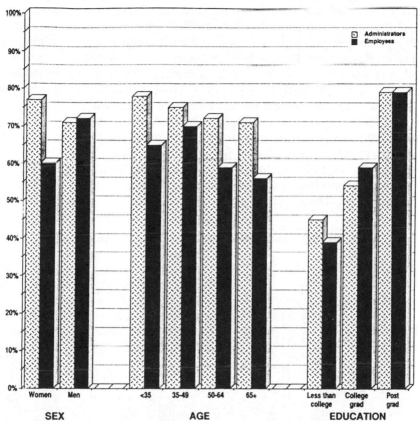

at least 60% of administrators in all fields valued sabbaticals. For employees and administrators, the opportunity for sabbaticals was more highly valued by those who rated their current educational benefits (Q.3e) as "fair" or "poor" than by those who rated them highly. Administrators who did not agree that they should always submit to church teaching (Q.14e) were more likely to value sabbaticals, but this relationship did not exist for employees.

In general, the employees' and administrators' answers to Question 12c (the importance of educational opportunities) parallel their answers to Question 12a on sabbaticals. Women, younger respondents and those with college or post-college education valued educational opportunities more highly than did men, respondents over 50, and those without college degrees. Diocesan workers rated educational opportunities less important than did workers for religious congregations or parishes. However, parish employees were more likely to value educational opportunities than they had been to value sabbaticals. Of all the categories surveyed, priests, both as administrators and as employees, were the least likely to consider educational opportunities very or fairly important. Still, even among the priests, over 70% valued these opportunities. Men and women religious administrators, women religious employees, lay employees and deacons were the most likely to value education. For all but the longest-employed administrators, the value of educational opportunities increased with length of employment; for employees the opposite was true. Table 2 summarizes these tendencies.

There are several possible reasons for these patterns, which could not be investigated with the current survey data. The oldest or the long-est-employed respondents were not asked if they had already had oppor-tunities for sabbaticals and continuing education; if they had indeed en-joyed such benefits in the past, this may explain their relative lack of interest now. The survey question on sabbaticals also did not specify

Table 1A
% Saying Sabbaticals "Very" or "Fairly" Important

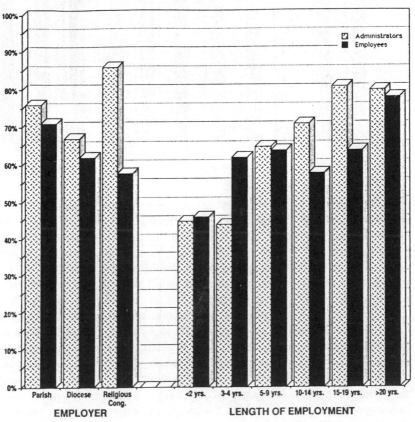

Table 2
% Saying Educational Opportunities "Very" or "Fairly" Important

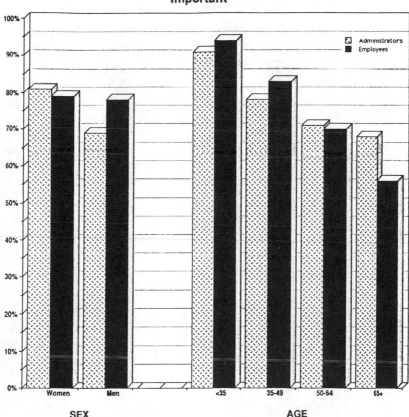

whether such time would be compensated at full salary or not, so respondents may have had differing concepts in mind when they answered it.

Q.3e and Q.12c Rating of Educational Benefits and The Importance of Educational Opportunities

Overall, only 33% of the employees and 21% of the administrators rated their educational benefits as either good or excellent. However, 81% of employees and 76% of administrators stated that the opportunity for further education was either fairly or very important to them. Looking at these two questions, it can be assumed that those employees who said that continuing their education was important (Q.12c), and yet at the same time reported that the educational benefits currently being offered to them were fair, poor, or nonexistent (Q.3e), would be dissatisfied with this aspect of working for the church. For administrators, the

Table 2A
% Saying Educational Opportunities "Very" or "Fairly" Important

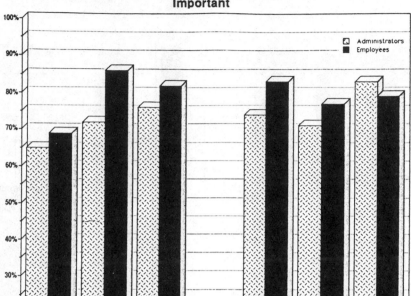

wording of Q.3e was somewhat different, asking the administrators to rate 'the benefits that *workers* are now receiving from the Church" and not the benefits of the administrator personally. If it is assumed that the administrators were applying this question to their own situations, then it can be inferred that the same dissatisfaction existed among the administrators who held education to be "important" or "very important" (Q.12c) and yet ranked workers' educational benefits "fair," "poor," or "do not have" (Q.3e).

When using this combined measure, a substantial proportion of both administrators and employees were dissatisfied with their current educational benefits: 385 of the 659 administrators (58.4%) and 335 of the 636 employees (52.6%). This is a serious finding for those who are dissatisfied with their educational benefits are far more likely to have thought of leaving church employment. When dissatisfaction with benefits was broken down by various categories of *employees.* there was no

Table 2B
% Saying Educational Opportunities "Very" or "Fairly" Important

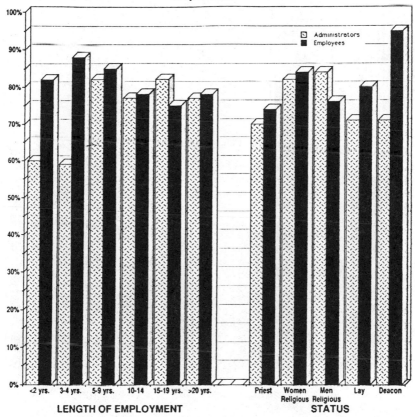

significant difference in the amount of dissatisfaction between male and female respondents, between the recently-hired and the long-term employees, between those working for parishes, dioceses or religious congregations, or between employees of different statuses (although priests expressed less dissatisfaction than the other categories in this last comparison). For *administrators,* on the other hand, all of these dimensions showed statistically significant differences: women administrators were more dissatisfied with their educational benefits than men, long-term administrators were more dissatisfied than recently-hired ones, administrators in parishes and religious congregations were more dissatisfied than diocesan administrators, and priests and married administrators with children were less dissatisfied than religious, single parents, married administrators without children and single administrators. On the other hand, there was a significant difference in dissatisfaction among employees who worked in different fields, with employees

Table 3
% Dissatisfied with Education Opportunities (Employees)

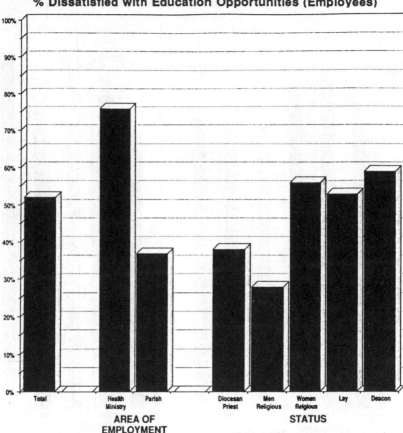

in health ministries most likely to be dissatisfied and parish employees least. For administrators differences in dissatisfaction by field were barely significant. For both employees and administrators, diocesan priests were significantly *less* dissatisfied with their educational benefits, women religious and lay respondents were more dissatisfied, and deacons were *more* dissatisfied if they were employees and less dissatisfied if they were administrators. No significant difference in dissatisfaction existed for either employees or administrators between respondents in various age groups or between those with more or less education. Table 3 summarizes these findings.

DISCUSSION

The current study's findings that women and younger administrators were more interested in education replicates the results of other

Table 3A
% Dissatisfied with Education Opportunities (Administrators)

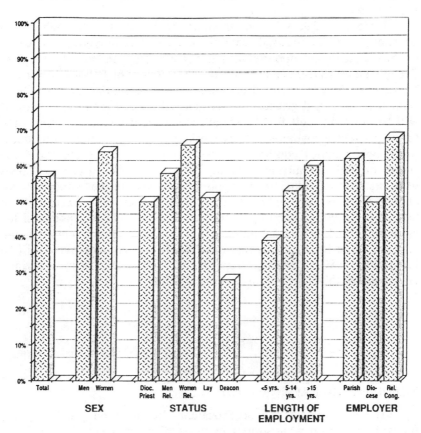

studies. (Hay Group, p.III-4; Dudley, 1990:4,6) These findings, however, do not address the question of *why* certain categories of respondents should express more interest in education. If the Labor Process
theorists are correct, however, one might speculate that those groups of
workers who are excluded from higher line positions in the church's
bureaucratic structure (i.e. from the top administrative posts in dioceses
and the role of pastor in parishes) may attempt to use their educational
credentials to gain a voice in decision-making. (La Magdeleine
1986:323) The fact that the *least* organizationally powerful groups—
women, the lay employee and the young—are the *most* interested in
education would support this thesis. The Human Relations theory, on
the other hand, is supported by the findings that long-term employees
value educational opportunities more than recently hired ones, and that
better-educated respondents desire still more educational opportunities.
If education is indeed a key to increasing employee satisfaction and

motivation, then one might expect that long-term and highly educated workers, whom studies have shown to be the most satisfied and motivated, would desire still more.

Whichever theory is true, it cannot be denied that the high dissatisfaction levels among both administrators and employees with regard to their educational opportunities is a cause for concern. As the Hay Group's study (p.II-7) and that of the Department of Labor (Bolick and Nestleroth, 1988:15) pointed out, future age cohorts of workers will be smaller in size, and greater competition will exist for their services. It will be more difficult for the church to hire and retain workers in the future particularly women and lay workers if dissatisfaction with educational opportunities continues at the current levels. As the telephone survey of Catholic laity not working for the institutional church shows, 96% stated that educational opportunities should be important for church workers, yet only 31.5% ranked the church "excellent" or "good" in providing such opportunities. It is unlikely that potential lay applicants holding these opinions will consider church employment. And yet given fewer priests it is more likely that lay employees will be hired. The NACPA findings reported in this section pose a definite challenge for the church in the coming decade.

PROMOTION

THEORETICAL BACKGROUND

The sociological and organizational literature on promotion has focused chiefly on what groups or types of persons are promoted and why. Ideally, promotion within an organization should be based on seniority and/ or expertise, selecting the most qualified occupant of the next lower positions to move to the subsequent level. This impartial process is a key mechanism for insuring commitment to the organization and motivates workers toward higher performance as they compete with each other for upward mobility. Recent researchers have pointed out, however, that the promotion process is always biased in favor of some groups and excludes others. A "Dual Labor Market" is common whereby the upper-level, "primary sector" jobs are restricted to the limited number of candidates who have the requisite credentials—whether or not these credentials actually reflect the ability of those who possess them. (Collins, 1979; Fallows, 1985) Primary labor market jobs are stable and better paid and offer possibilities for upward mobility. "Workers in the secondary sector, by contrast, are poorly paid, and their employment is episodic or seasonal. There is little chance for career advancement, and few opportunities to move into the primary sector."

(Wittberg, 1989a, p.287. See also Salaman, 1981:109-110) The corporate secretaries described by Kanter are a good example of secondary labor market employees:

> The secretarial ladder was short, and rank was determined by bosses' statuses. A survey of 88 [secretaries] at one location in 1974 indicated just how limited the secretarial/clerical opportunity structure was. Though 25% of the women had worked for the company over 15 years, only 12% had held more than 3 jobs in the corporation. An old hand recalled: "A person used to be 45 before becoming an executive secretary and stayed there for 15 to 20 years. Now . . . they get there at 29 and have no place else to go." Salaries were also not high. Over half of the women earned less than $11,000 a year, despite so many with long service. (Kanter, 1977:71)

In contrast, for the primary sector, promotion was THE most important aspect of the job:

> It was hard for success to mean anything else but movement in a large hierarchical organization like Indsco. The incentives were all for mobility. Long service or good continuing performance took a distinct back seat. . . Good work got a person a salary and the standard 15% in benefits. But there were upper limits on pay within a job classification, and after a time, good performance could only be rewarded through promotion. (Kanter, 1977:129)

In other words, one important aspect of the promotion process in any organization is the extent to which some employees within the organization are confined to secondary labor market "ghettoes" and excluded from mobility into the better-paid, more secure, more powerful positions.

Another potential conflict arises around the relative importance of merit vs. seniority as determining criteria for promotion. As several researchers of both church-related and non-church-related organizations have pointed out, (Peterson and Schoenherr, 1978:818; Schoenherr and Sorenson, 1982:44; Reese, 1989:227-28; Hodson and Sullivan, 1990:160, 270), seniority is most important in organizations where there is little financial remuneration and where it is difficult to establish objective and measurable merit criteria. Still another aspect to be considered is that the structural opportunities for promotion vary in different types of organizations. An organization with few upper-level "slots" into which people can be promoted may have trouble motivating its employees, since they will see themselves as stuck in dead-end jobs. If the organization attempts to create more upper-level positions to combat this, a form of "organizational inflation" may develop. The value of each position becomes devalued and, at the same time, the organization becomes top-heavy with managerial personnel. (Kanter, 1977:163; Hodson and Sullivan, 1990:187)

A final consideration is the distinction between staff and line positions. Line positions are those whose occupants are eligible for promotion to higher levels of supervision. Occupants of staff positions, while nominally of the same rank as line administrators, provide a particular service or have a particular, limited area of expertise. They are, therefore, assumed to be lacking the wide-ranging experience necessary for upper management and so are rarely considered for promotion beyond their department. Thus, a company may draw its executives from the middle management in sales or finance and not from personnel or computer services. Minorities and women more often occupy staff positions, which then become the "black slot" or the "women's slot."

RESEARCH ON CHURCH WORKERS

Priests

Researchers have generally agreed that there are two separate career tracks within the diocesan priesthood in the United States. This was observed in research two decades ago, and does not seem to have changed in recent studies. (Hall and Schneider, 1973; Dahm, 1981:46-52; Peterson and Schoenherr, 1978:813-16; Reese, 1989:224) Occupants of the "fast track" are chosen while still in the seminary and sent to institutes such as the North American College in Rome. Upon graduation, they move into full-time chancery or other diocesan positions. The average age of chancery priests, at least through the 1970's, was thus younger than the average age of pastors. After chancery service, these priests moved directly to pastor large parishes, and, if all went well, some were chosen to become bishops or other high officials. The decision of which seminarians to assign to which track does not seem to depend on such background factors as the socio-economic status of one's parents, which is often used to screen out lower class members from the top positions in other organizations. In this instance, the church is more egalitarian in its promotion policies than most institutions. The only factor which exerted a slight positive effect on a seminarian's chances of being put on the fast track at least in previous decades is Irish ancestry. The proportion of bishops of Irish descent is larger than the percentage of Irish descended clergy, which, in turn, is larger than the percentage of Irish-descended American Catholics. (Peterson and Schoenherr, 1978:807, 812; Szafran, 1980:44-45; Sandoval, 1990:80)

Priests in the other, slower career track attended the diocesan seminary, spent several years as associates at various parishes, and then were appointed to their first positions as pastor in small rural parishes and "worked their way up" to large, wealthy urban or suburban parishes. The length of time spent as an associate has varied: until the 1970's, it could have been as long as 25 to 30 years (Kantowicz, 1983; Hall and Schneider, 1973). Today, Reese reports (1989:224) that the time spent before receiving one's own parish ranges from 1.5 to 25 years in different U.S. dioceses. Promotion within the second track is based on seniority alone (Hall and Schneider, 1973:30; Peterson and Schoenhen, 1978:807; Reese, 1989:227-228), despite the fact that 78% of the priests Scheets studied said they preferred promotion based on ability. (Scheets, 1989a:6) Thus, the inherent conflict between promotion based on seniority and that based on merit, which occurs in all organizations, is especially keenly felt by priests. (Peterson and Schoenherr, 1978:797)

This promotion process may have several negative implications, both for the institutional church and for the individual priest. Hall and Schneider (1973: Chapt. 8) and Kim (1979:98) reported that assistants who must wait several decades before becoming pastors tend to have low organizational commitment and to become discouraged. This situation has improved a little in recent years, especially in those dioceses where the wait for one's own parish is short and where the small number of associates insures that they have greater voice in their assignments. (Reese, 1989:22) In dioceses with numerous priests and a longer waiting period before appointment as pastor, priests may still "have little control over [their] own life's development in the priesthood," a situation unchanged since the early 1970's. (Hall and Schneider, 1973:221)

Another difficulty used to be the transition from associate to pastor. Hall and Schneider (1973: Chapt. 5) found that associates had very little responsibility in their first assignments that could have prepared them for the experience of running their own parishes later. The transition was especially difficult if the new pastor was alone in a rural area where he was "on call" 24 hours a day precisely the most likely first solo assignment. This problem was not addressed in more recent literature, so there is little information as to whether transition to pastor difficulties still exist.

A final difficulty, at least in former times, was the flatness of the promotion ladder in the second career track. By the age of 50 or so, there were no further upward moves to make. Priests moved to the most valued parishes (usually the largest and wealthiest ones) by their mid-50's, and stayed there an average of 27 years, effectively blocking upward movement by those behind them. (Kantowicz, 1980) Peterson and Schoenhel (1978:807) found that, after the age of 50, neither more education nor more seniority gained the priest a better position. Of course, Peterson's and Schoenherr's data were gathered before the onset of the priest shortage. It would be interesting to investigate whether these patterns still exist.

Religious and Lay Workers

According to a recent study, priests hold 64% of the top 19 diocesan jobs. Lay men hold 18%, mostly in finance and administration. Women (religious and lay together) hold 16%, concentrated in traditionally female areas such as education. (Conscience, 1988:3) Of the top diocesan positions in 1988, lay men and women comprised 3% of chancellors, 8% of vice chancellors, and fewer than 1% of tribunal judges. Women religious comprised 11% of the chancellors, 10% of the vice chancellors, and 1% of the tribunal judges. (Conscience, 1988:67) The rest of these positions were held by priests. Over 91% of the directors of finance and administration were male (56% lay; 30% priests), as were 90% of the finance council positions (56% lay and 33% priests). (Conscience, 1988:9) In education, women religious accounted for 45% of the superintendents of schools and 48% of the religious education directors. Lay men occupied 20% and 18% of these positions and lay women 7% and 11%. (Conscience, 1988:10) As Heslin, (1983:4) and several other authors have stated, "women religious are severely underrepresented according to their numbers in administration levels beyond the parish." (See also Rosenberg and Sullivan, 1980:77) The laity, of course, are even more under-represented.

Within dioceses and parishes, women religious usually occupy staff positions such as director of religious education, rather than line positions such as chancellor or parish administrator. Rosenberg and Sullivan's data (1980:75) show that 65% of the respondents were classified as "professional" (i.e.as providing a specialized service) and only 25% as "managerial." And when women religious do occupy managerial positions, they are canonically barred from advancing to bishop or ordained pastor. This ceiling on their promotion may be especially distressing to women religious, many of whom had been accustomed to the relatively open promotional ladders in their own institutions prior to beginning work for dioceses and parishes. (Heslin, 1983:115; Wittberg, 1989b:15-67; Wittberg, 1989c:534)

A similar process also seems to happen to women ministers in Protestant churches. Carroll (1982:150) found that it was difficult for women to rise through line positions and become senior pastors, so they tended to remain as assistants (often in charge of religious education or youth ministry), or to move into staff positions in their denomination's regional administration. Those women who did become the sole pastors of a church tended to remain in rural or marginal parishes. (Carroll, 1982:129)

RESULTS OF THE CURRENT STUDY

Q.12e: Promotion Opportunities

As would be expected, promotion opportunities were ranked either very or fairly important by 70% of the employees and 61% of the administrators. For both employees and administrators, women held promotion opportunities to be more important than men did, and younger respondents (under 35) valued promotion opportunities more than older ones (over 50). These patterns replicate patterns found among employees and administrators in non-church-related organizations. (Hay Group III-4) There were also some more specific patterns unique to this study. Recently hired respondents and those working between 5 and 9 years tended to think promotion most important. Male religious, priests and deacons ranked promotion least important, while lay respondents

Table 4
% Saying Promotion Opportunities "Very" or "Fairly"
Important

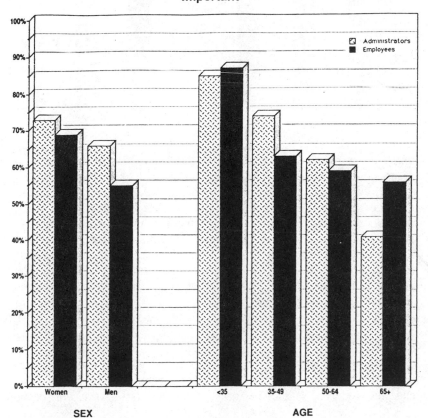

Table 4A
% Saying Promotion Opportunities "Very" or "Fairly" Important

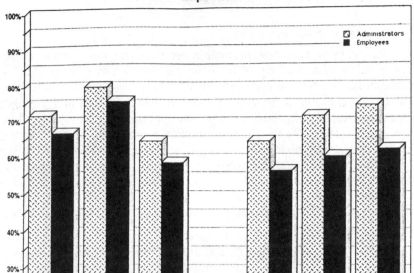

and women religious were the most likely to value it. For *employees*, respondents with some college or a college degree were significantly more likely to value promotion opportunities, but the differences between education levels were not significant for administrators. Administrators who were married and single parent administrators were more likely to think promotion important. Finally, employees in charities, health and youth ministry ranked promotion opportunities more important; employees in parishes least. This difference was not significant among administrators. For both employees and administrators, there was no significant relationship between the importance of promotion opportunities and whether the respondent worked for a diocesan office, a parish, or a religious congregation. Table 4 summarizes these differences.

For employees there was a statistically significant relationship between the value placed on promotion opportunities and whether the respondent received regular performance evaluations. Those who received such evaluations were more likely to say promotion opportunities were important. Also, those who thought promotion opportunities important were more likely to rate their salary comparability as poor.

Table 4B
% Saying Promotion Opportunities "Very" or "Fairly"
Important

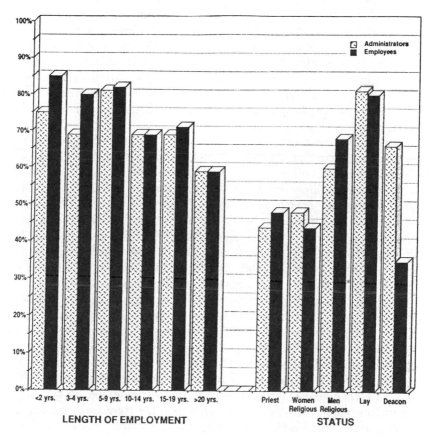

Q.12e and Q.6d: Satisfaction with Promotion Opportunities

Many respondents, both employees and administrators, (112 of the 641 employees and 202 of the 662 administrators) said that promotion opportunities were important to them (Q.12e), but that they had become discouraged because the restrictive rules of the church denied them the opportunity to grow and work in its service (Q.6d). This question was the closest analog in the survey to perceiving limitations on promotion. (Please note that, as with Q.3e in the preceding section of this report, the same difference occurs between the employees' and the administrators' question wording: the administrators' question asks whether *workers in general* have become discouraged.) Since employees and administrators for whom promotion opportunities were the most important were also the most likely to have thought of finding a job elsewhere, it seemed advisable to construct a special variable measuring dissatisfaction with promotion opportunities: if a respondent stated that such opportunities were very or fairly important to him/her in Question 12e, and yet expressed discouragement about church restrictions on professional growth in Question 6d, he/she was considered to be dissatisfied with promotion opportunities in the church.

For both employees and administrators, dissatisfaction with promotion opportunities was not significantly related to educational level or to length of employment. No category of these two dimensions was more likely to be dissatisfied with promotion opportunities than any other. However, for administrators, women were more likely to be dissatisfied with their promotion opportunities than men were, women religious more dissatisfied than priests and deacons, and single parents and married administrators more dissatisfied than priests and singles. None of these relationships was as pronounced for employees. On the other hand, employees between the ages of 25 and 34 and those who worked for charities, youth ministry and diocesan offices were more dissatisfied with their promotion opportunities; this relationship did not hold true for administrators. For administrators (but not for employees), respondents who worked for religious congregations were more likely to express dissatisfaction with promotion opportunities.

When dissatisfaction with promotion opportunities was compared across parishes, dioceses and religious congregations for each state in life separately, the men and women religious, both employees and administrators working for religious congregations, no longer showed a significant difference in dissatisfaction when compared to those working for parishes or dioceses. Lay administrators also showed no significant difference across the three employers, but lay employees in diocesan offices were much more dissatisfied and lay employees in religious congregations much *less* dissatisfied, than lay employees elsewhere. It would therefore seem that the concentration of dissatisfaction with promotion opportunities among administrators in religious congregations is due chiefly to the large number of women religious who work there, since, as was seen above, women religious administrators tend to be more dissatisfied with their promotion opportunities.

Diocesan priests were the least dissatisfied of all the status categories. However, among priest administrators, those who worked for dioceses were significantly more satisfied with their promotion opportunities than those priest administrators (pastors) who worked for parishes, a possible confirmation of the two-track system reported above. Among priest employees, however, this difference was not significant.

Q.9: Promotion of Minorities

For both employees and administrators, the evaluation of the church's record in promoting minorities was related to their own evaluation of how important promotion opportunities were. Those who felt that promotion opportunities were important were significantly less likely to rate the church as "excellent" (and significantly more likely to rate it "fair" or "poor") in promoting blacks and other minorities. Administrators who felt that promotion opportunities were important were also more likely to rate the church as poor at promoting the disabled, but the employees' answers, while tending in the same direction, were not statistically significant.

As was noted in the summary of the NACPA attitude survey, women administrators and employees were significantly less likely than men to rate the church as "good" or "excellent" in promoting women. When analyzed separately, both men and women administrators showed no significant relationship between the value they themselves placed on promotion opportunities and their rating of the church's record in promoting women. For male *employees,* however, there was a slight tendency to replicate the pattern given above with regard to other minorities (i.e. for the male employees who considered promotion opportunities important to be more likely to rate the church as poor on promoting women.)

DISCUSSION

A strong reservoir of dissatisfaction exists, especially among the laity and women religious, with promotion opportunities in the church. This dissatisfaction is potentially quite serious, since employees and administrators who are dissatisfied with their promotion opportunities are much more likely to have thought of looking for a job elsewhere. Women administrators and employees, especially, are aware of the church's record in promoting women. And priests are not immune to dissatisfaction. As both Hall and Schneider (1973) and Hoge (1987:112-113) would have predicted, diocesan priests administering parishes (i.e. pastors), who had reached the probable end point of their careers on the slow track, were more dissatisfied than priest administrators working in "fast track" positions in diocesan offices. In the future, the church will have to address the promotion concerns of both its lay and its ordained employees, or risk losing them to outside positions. Furthermore, since, according to the telephone survey of Catholic laity not working for the institutional church, 87.4% of this group also believe that promotional opportunities for church employees are either very or fairly important, improvement of the public perception of the church's record in this area is necessary if the church is to be competitive in attracting new and qualified employees in the coming period of labor shortages.

CONCLUSION

The survey questions discussed here present a challenging agenda for the church. With regard to educational opportunities, a majority of both the administrators and the employees interviewed are dissatisfied with the benefits currently offered by the church. This dissatisfaction is greatest among precisely those categories of respondents upon whom the church will have to rely more heavily as sources of future personnel: women and the laity in general. Valuable long term administrators were also more dissatisfied, a disquieting sign, since the respondents most dissatisfied with educational opportunities were the most likely to be thinking of leaving church employment. Even among priests, the least dissatisfied group, the youngest priests hold education to be the most important. In a time of shrinking financial contributions (Greeley and McManus, 1987), therefore, the church will somehow have to find the resources to provide better educational opportunities for its employees.

Similarly, the current near-monopoly of top diocesan administrative positions by ordained priests is discouraging to many of the lay respondents. Moving priests out of these positions and back to parish work, however, is likely to increase *their* dissatisfaction, since pastors are already more dissatisfied with their promotion opportunities than are priests in diocesan offices. (See also Hoge, 1987:112) These challenges present NACPA with a valuable agenda in the coming years, since much further study and consultation will be needed to remedy some of these difficulties.

Job Descriptions, Performance Appraisals, Recruitment

JOB CLARITY AND PERFORMANCE APPRAISAL

THEORETICAL BACKGROUND

One of the chief characteristics of most twentieth-century organizations is their conformity to bureaucratic models and processes. According to Max Weber, bureaucratically organized groups can be distinguished from pre-bureaucratic or non-bureaucratic ones by their carefully delineated distribution of tasks and responsibilities among the group members. Ideally, each worker and each administrator in an office, a factory, a hospital and (increasingly) a church has a written description of the perimeters of his/her job, and is hired and promoted solely on the basis of his/her ability in carrying out these particular functions. Such a rational basis of organization, Weber felt, contributed to the superior efficiency of the bureaucratic form over previous models as far superior "as machine manufacture is over nonmechanical modes of production." (Weber, 1984:31)

Not all students of organizations are in agreement with Weber about the superiority of bureaucracies. Much recent attention has been given to the concept of worker cooperatives as alternatives to the bureaucratic organization of businesses. (See, for example, Hunnius, 1973; Bernstein, 1976; McManus, 1987) The 1960's were an especially fertile period for the founding of such ventures. But the majority of the so-called cooperatives today are in fact merely *owned* by the workers through Employee Stock Ownership Plans (ESOP's). "The fact that employees have purchased their workplace is a far cry from saying that they control it; in fact, it doesn't necessarily mean the employees have any voice in the decisions at all." (Zwerdling, 1984:5) Most attempts at true cooperative organizations fail, because of the efficiency disadvantage which cooperatives have when compared to bureaucracies. As one member of a failed garment factory cooperative commented:

> I don't believe a coop can work. There has to be a boss. There has to be someone who makes people do things even if they don't want to, no matter how much they holler and get angry about it. People are followers. (Zwerdling, 1984:12)

Despite this rather pessimistic assessment, some successful worker cooperatives have flourished, notably the Mondragon cooperatives in Spain and the plywood cooperatives of the Pacific Northwest. (Gutierrez and Whyte, 1976; Zwerdling, 1984:95) Still, most businesses in this country and elsewhere in the industrialized West are bureaucratized, if for no other reason than that the members of their surrounding culture expect them to be, and often will not take them seriously otherwise. (Meyer and Rowan, 1980) At times, this pressure to bureaucratize affects organizations that would be better off under a more cooperative model.

Even the most bureaucratized organizations, however, are seldom organized in a purely bureaucratic manner. This is because, paradoxically, the delimitation of an employee's job by a job description and various accompanying regulations actually gives a large amount of power to that worker. Crozier (1964), for example, has shown how the workers in a French factory were able to use the factory rules and job descriptions to neutralize practically all of management's discretionary authority over their work lives. (See also Perrow, 1986:24) Because of the limitations which articulated job descriptions place on their power, managers have often resisted providing them for subordinates. As Kanter observed:

> Within the general constraints of Indsco tradition and the practice of other managers, bosses had enormous personal latitude around secretaries. The absence of job descriptions . . . meant that there was no way to insure some uniformity of demands across jobs with the same general outlines . . . Thus, it was left to bosses to determine what secretaries did, how they spent their time and whether they were to be given opportunities for movement. There was no such thing as career reviews for secretaries... (Kanter, 1977:78)

Similarly, Ingram (1980) noted that Baptist ministers strongly resisted drawing up job descriptions for parish employees, since this would have limited their own power. And similar practices have been observed in Catholicism:

> Though he regularized procedures for building and finance, centralized decision-making in various areas, and created several new diocesan agencies, [Mundelein] kept bureaucracy to

a minimum. No personnel board advised him, no civil service-type standards guided him in making appointments; instead he gained and kept control by carefully selecting "his men" and placing them in positions of importance. (Kantowicz, 1983:150)

What distinguished the church was not centralization but the lack of accountability (no board of directors), the secrecy, not only from the public but even within the administration . . . and the failure to develop rational procedures . . . *in short the absence, not the presence, of bureaucracy.* Cardinals O'Connell, Mundelein and Spellman thought they were imitating the best practices of American business, but their rule partook far more of . . . the inefficiency of Louis XIV than the workings of a large scale business enterprise in industrial society. (O'Brien 1989:10) [Italics mine]

The question of job descriptions and performance appraisals, therefore, is central to a study of church employment. Unclear job descriptions and the lack of specified accountability procedures may result in inefficiency at best and abuses of power over employees at worst. On the other hand, overbureaucratization through too compartmentalized areas of responsibility may prove equally alienating.

RESEARCH ON CHURCH WORKERS

Ministerial Staff Positions Within the Catholic Church

The Catholic Church as a whole, and the Catholic parish in particular, has not been exempt from the trend toward bureaucratization in the larger society, whether or not this is always desirable. (Meyer and Rowan, 1980) Concomitant characteristics of bureaucratic organizations such as the proliferation of specialized positions have begun to develop, and there is at least the assumption that each position encompasses a specific area of responsibility and expertise for which a job description could be written. The Notre Dame study of parish life (NCCB, 1982) found that 23% of U.S. parishes have permanent deacons, 30% have lay people in professional roles, 33% have sisters in non school parish ministry, 31% have sisters in religious education, and 44% have sisters in parochial schools. (55% have schools; the other 11% are staffed entirely by lay employees) On the other hand, half of all U.S. parishes have only one person, the pastor, on staff. (NCCB, 1982:25) Table 1, reprinted from the Notre Dame study, lists the frequency of some organized parish activities. Many, although not all, of these are the responsibility of some specifically hired parish staff person.

Table 1
Frequency of Some Organized Parish Activities

Activity	Pct. of Parishes
Liturgy Planning	72.2
Ministry to the Sick	70.7
Adult Religious Education	63.3
Youth Ministry	62.4
Ministry to the Elderly	58.6
Social Service	51.6
Music/Other Cultural Activities	49.4
Marriage/Family Development	48.0
Prayer Groups	45.9
Ministry Training	36.7
Evangelization	31.7
Catechumenate	31.5
Charismatic Renewal	23.2
Social Action	20.0
Ministry to Divorced/Separated	19.8

These data mean that, today, pastors must supervise an ever growing parish staff. A study of parishes in Indianapolis found that the average parish had one priest, one other paid professional (lay or religious), 1.4 support staff (secretaries, housekeeper), and one maintenance worker. (Archdiocese of Indianapolis, 1984:11) Scheets' study of parishes in Elizabeth, NJ, found that the average pastor supervised 4.4 supporting staff members. (Scheets, 1989a:10) On the diocesan level, too, offices, agencies and secretariats have multiplied. Increasingly, these offices are staffed by lay employees.

There are several tensions and dilemmas implicit in the multiplication of staff positions in increasingly bureaucratized church ministries. First of all, there is a tension between bureaucratization as a value on the one hand and bureaucratization as a deadening force on the other. Bureaucratic practices such as job descriptions and performance evaluations can be beneficial: Joseph (1982:6), cites the need to define work roles within parish staff positions and thus reduce role conflict/strain. A major complaint of the parish workers studied by Wittberg (1989b) was the lack of job descriptions and job clarity. Since, as was pointed out above, employees can use job descriptions and performance appraisals as a potential safeguard against possibly arbitrary actions or abrupt dismissals by their employers, it is not surprising that staff workers in parishes and dioceses prefer to have them.

On the other hand, there is a certain amount of evidence that parish functioning is not amenable to division into separate, formally articulated tasks. The Notre Dame study found that the more effective parishes were more widely participative in form: compared to less effective parishes, they were more likely to have a team style of leadership (69% to 35%), frequent staff meetings (80% to 60%), parish councils (89% to 77%), and more active use of lay people (54% to 30%). (NCCB, 1982:30. See also Carroll, 1982:201) In short, bureaucratization through the multiplication of staff roles and job descriptions can stifle the active involvement of "non-professionals" in the parish, in favor of the one individual whose job description mandates a given responsibility. It must also be admitted, however, that the *non bureaucratic* form of organization in which the pastor does not delegate any tasks can also stifle this involvement.

A second tension, on the diocesan level, involves what Kim (1979:98) called the split between hierarchy and agency, a parallel to the line/staff division. The Notre Dame study observed that, since Vatican II, a second tier of diocesan offices has been created, comprising such functions as religious education, social action, personnel, housing, liturgy, ethnic concerns and the like. (NCCB, 1982:41) These offices are more frequently staffed and administered by lay persons, and often are not well-integrated with the canonical and institutional offices. More recently, there has been a movement in some dioceses to consolidate the two tiers into secretariats, but there is still the danger of a staff line split, with the second tier (staff) jobs being held by women religious and the laity and remaining "dead ends" relative to the canonical (line) positions held by the clergy.

Table 2
Ratio of Priests (Ministers) to People

	Catholics	Episcopalians	Lutherans	Methodists
1965	1/750	1/350	1/426	1/451
1975	1/827	1/235	1/360	1/389
1985	1/917	1/196	1/247	1/340

The current decrease in the numbers of priests compounds the strains already posed by this multiplication of bureaucratic church positions and by the increasing reliance on lay employees to fill them. Hoge, Carroll and Scheets report (1988:34) that the number of Catholics per priest is rising while comparable Protestant denominations have seen their ratios fall:

> Priests are also unevenly distributed between dioceses: Los Angeles has one priest for every 1892 Catholics; Detroit one for every 1452, and New York one for every 745. (Hoge,

1987:107) Current indications are that the priest shortage will
become worse in future decades. By 2000, 38% of the active
diocesan clergy will be over 55; in 1970 only 23% were. (See
also Schoenherr et al, 1988:501; Hoge et al, 1988:268-69;
Hoge 1987:Chapter 1; and Catholic Church Personnel in the
U.S. 1984) The evidence is also that a large influx of young
seminarians is unlikely. Scheets (1989a:7) found that only
64% of the priests he surveyed would recommend their life-
style to potential recruits. Since several researchers (Greeley,
1972a: 268; Hoge, 1983:38) have found that the single most
influential factor in a young man's decision to become a
priest is encouragement by current priests, the reluctance of
priests to recommend their life-style would seem to preclude a
reversal of the vocation decline in the near future.

Three difficulties result from this situation. First of all, the declining number of priests means that an increasing number of lay persons
will be hired to perform various functions within parishes and dioceses.
As several studies have pointed out (Hay Group, p. 117; Bolick and
Nestleroth, 1988:310), there is an approaching demographic slump in
the number of young potential employees who will be graduating from
high school and college in the 1990's: two million (8%) fewer than in
previous decades. This scarcity will render such workers more expensive, precisely at a time when, as Greeley and McManus (1987) point
out, the financial contributions of Catholics to the church are declining.
Lay workers will also demand the sort of job descriptions, promotion
opportunities, and decision-making input that their experiences in other,
secular organizations have led them to expect.

A second difficulty results from the fact that, traditionally, chancery positions were part of the "fast track" of clergy careers. Hall and
Schneider (1973) found that such positions had more status and that the
priests who held them were more satisfied with their ministry. The increased prestige of diocesan chancery positions seems to have continued to the present day. Hoge (1987:112-113) found that over 50% of
the priests he surveyed said that they would not want to leave these
positions and concentrate solely on sacramental ministry. Even in a
time of fewer priests, therefore, priests are likely to resist surrendering
chancery positions to nonclergy.

Some dioceses have attempted to recruit priests from other countries. This decision, however, has several liabilities, some of which the
U.S. Church has experienced before. The present priest shortage is not
unique in church history. Dolan (1987:16) notes that, in the late 1800's,
the U.S. averaged one priest for every 1,167 Catholics. In Manhattan at
that time, there was one priest for every *4000* Catholics. The nineteenth
century priest shortage reduced the bishop's authority over individual
priests; immigrants imported their own priests, and foreign priests could

"diocese shop" for more favorable conditions. So, in the first half of the twentieth century, bishops made a deliberate attempt to reduce their reliance on foreign priests and to increase the number of locally-trained clergy. (Kantowicz, 1983:49)

Moreover, recruiting immigrant priests is even less satisfactory today than it was in the nineteenth century. Whereas immigrant priests at that time were similar in culture to the immigrants they served, twentieth century immigrant priests are not. Hoge (1987:118) documents culture shock and adaptation difficulties on the part of priests from India, Africa and other developing countries when dealing with American Catholics. For this reason, many dioceses have restricted this option for alleviating the shortage of diocesan priests. (Hoge, 1987:118)

For the foreseeable future, therefore, the research appears to indicate that more and more lay workers will be needed on both the parish and the diocesan level. These workers will, however, be harder to attract and to retain, given the projected shortage of persons to fill entry-level jobs (Bolick and Nestleroth, 1988) and the comparative unattractiveness of the educational and promotion opportunities attached to some positions in the institutional church. And the parishes and dioceses which do hire more lay workers will find it necessary to provide job descriptions and performance evaluations for them, since these procedures are expected in other organizations. Currently, many positions remain in the institutional church for which job descriptions and performance evaluations do not exist, especially on the parish level. (Kinsella, 1989: 2022; Branagan, 1990:5)

JOB DESCRIPTIONS AND PERFORMANCE APPRAISALS

Priests

The idea of having job descriptions and performance appraisals for priests and other Church workers is a comparatively recent one, although one for which there is much support. Scheets (1989a 11-16), for example, found that 80% of the Elizabeth priests and 69% of the New England priests he studied favored performance appraisals. Neither job descriptions nor performance appraisals are common for priests in the church, nor are they well done when they do exist. (Kinsella, 1989:21-22; Reese, 1989:251-254) All levels of the clergy are short-changed in this regard: "the relationship between the pastor and his curate is the most poorly structured in the entire ecclesiastical administration. There is great uncertainty whether it should be interpreted along the lines of father/son, employer/employee, mentor/apprentice, or junior/senior colleague." (Dahm, 1981:12) The roles of permanent deacons are also unclear. Hoge, Carroll and Scheets (1988:17) point out that, according to the deacons they surveyed, there is little a deacon can do that the average lay person cannot. This leads, the authors said, to frustration and cynicism. On a diocesan level, Reese (1989:136-137) found that there were unclear job descriptions for regional vicars vis-a-vis the bishop's power, and that the vicar's role in performance appraisal and the promotion of the priests under him was undefined. (See also Dahm, 1982: chapter 5) At all levels, therefore, priests and deacons experience a lack of clearly articulated job descriptions.

With regard to performance appraisals for priests, several researchers have found a similarly distressing lack. According to Kinsella (1989:21), only 36% of dioceses had performance appraisals for their priests at all (as compared to 55% who said they had job descriptions for priests). Reese (1989:251) stated that, among those dioceses that did do performance appraisals, there was a lack of systematic appraisals of priests' work and an unwillingness of the appraisers to be direct. In part, this can be attributed to the difficulty of measuring successful performance in the priesthood. Blau states (1973: chapt. 3) that, when workers must be evaluated on their performance of essentially unmeasurable tasks, there is a strong tendency to substitute measurable tasks for the unmeasurable ones. Thus, more emphasis may be put on a pastor's ability to keep the parish accounts balanced than on his success in reaching out to the parishioners.

JOB DESCRIPTIONS AND PERFORMANCE APPRAISALS

Religious

According to Kinsella (1989:21), 83% of the religious working in U.S. dioceses have job descriptions; 50% said they also had regular performance appraisals. Especially in the new parish and diocesan-based ministries, however, job descriptions and performance appraisals are informal at best, rather than formally established in whatever contracts they had signed.

The studies are unanimous in agreeing that job clarity is a significant predictor of job satisfaction among the sisters working for parishes and dioceses. (Joseph, 1982:40; Wittberg, 1989b:151) The amorphous and ill-defined character of many church positions was especially stressful for women religious, because they had formerly worked in settings where they had job descriptions, mobility opportunities, and decision-making authority in short, in line positions within the bureaucratic structures of their own congregations or congregationally sponsored ministries. (According to Joseph, 1982:15, almost one-third of the sisters working in new parish and diocesan ministries had previously been part of congregational/regional administration.) The lack of job descriptions and the "secretary-like" dependence upon a pastor or an upper-level diocesan cleric, so characteristic of many staff positions in the church, was therefore especially difficult for them:

> As experienced women religious changed from a traditional administrative/line position as a principal to . . . a nontraditional ministry, they functioned more as staff persons to ordained men (clergy). Most [former] principals in this study enjoyed the power of initiating decisions. The challenge in a new ministry seemed to be the lack of a clear process for decision-making (Heslin 1983: 112)

The lack of job descriptions, therefore, reduced the authority of the sisters in parish ministry. As Joseph observed (1982:33), "these data strongly suggest what many have observed at the parish level—an ambiguity of function, over-lapping roles and a lack of clarity in job titles." The lack of regular performance appraisals also meant that the sisters' jobs were often quite tenuous. Coy (1988:5) points out that, even when contracts existed, a parish employee could be fired by the pastor without a stated reason by the simple expedient of refusing to renew the contract.

JOB DESCRIPTIONS AND PERFORMANCE APPRAISALS

Lay Employees

According to Kinsella (1989:21), 85% of lay church employees have job descriptions and 64% have performance appraisals regularly. These figures vary, however, by the location of the lay worker's employment. Only 62% of the 300 lay ministers in parish positions interviewed by Fox (1986) had job descriptions (only 60% had contracts). Only one half of La Magdeleine's respondents who were in charge of parish religious education had job descriptions. (La Magdeleine, 1986:322) One third of La Magdeleine's respondents had no budget. Similarly, only 37% of the lay DRE's had yearly performance appraisals (as compared to 53% of the religious DRE's). La Magdeleine states flatly that these jobs are secondary sector jobs in the church's dual labor market. (La Magdeleine, 1986:322) Fox cites the "insecurity and low salary of positions, and limited acceptance by priests, both as peers and for a range of functions" as chief sources of complaint by lay parish employees all characteristics of secondary labor market positions. (Fox, 1986:137)

This "lack of regularized accountability systems" for employees (Fox, 1986:214) is a source of strain and dissatisfaction. When Fox's survey asked for ways that their work situation could be improved, lay employees ranked "Efforts should be more valued" first and "Role should be clarified" second. (Fox, 1986:192) A similar situation exists for nonordained employees in local Protestant churches. Carroll (1982:39) found that the status of these lay professionals is "indeterminate and the salary [and prestige] is low." Often these employees have no vote in denominational policies, and no clearly articulated areas of responsibility: "In a society ever more specialized, in which job descriptions have become more and more explicit, professional roles for [lay women professionals] in the church are frustrating in their generality." (Carroll, 1982:40)

FINDINGS OF THE CURRENT STUDY

Q.7a: Job Clarity/Job Descriptions

It must be noted that the wording of Q.7a differs for administrators and employees. The administrators' questionnaire asked respondents to agree or disagree with the statement: "We give clear descriptions of job duties and functions for most positions." The corresponding question for employees was "I have a clear description of my job duties and functions." This difference in wording makes the responses comparable across employing agencies and fields. However, comparing employees and administrators across educational levels, life-styles, or the other demographic categories is not possible, since it is not evident in the data that (e.g.) college graduate administrators and college graduate employees worked in the same type of agency. This section will, therefore, compare the responses of employees and administrators with regard to place or field of employment and will next compare employees or administrators of one educational level or state in life with the employees or administrators of different educational levels or life-styles.

General agreement exists between employees and administrators working for dioceses on whether the employees have job descriptions. Approximately 70% of both groups agreed that they do. Employees and administrators working in diocesan offices, in education, and in health, youth ministry and charities also agreed on the existence of job descriptions for employees there, although the spread between employees' and administrators' answers was slightly wider. However, there was a significant difference between the responses of the administrators working in parishes (usually the pastor) and the employees working there. Parish employees were much less likely (12%) to say that they had clear job descriptions than the parish administrators were to say that they gave the descriptions. This finding replicates the findings of Joseph (1982), Fox (1986), Wittberg (1989b) and La Magdeleine (1986) that workers in parishes have a lack of clarity about their jobs. There was also a strong difference between the employees and administrators of religious congregations about the prevalence of job descriptions, but, in this case, the employees were more likely to say that they had job descriptions than the administrators were to say that they gave them. Table 3 summarizes these results.

TABLE 3
% With Job Descriptions

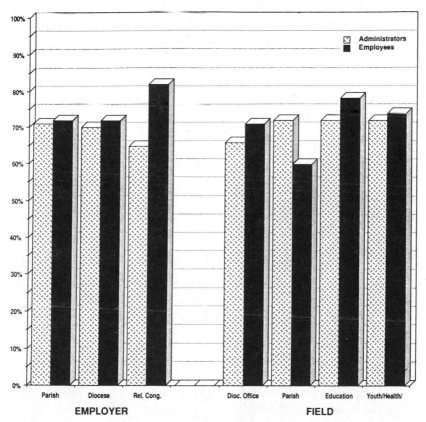

Among administrators, there was no significant difference between priests, religious and lay respondents in their assessment of whether or not employees had clear job descriptions. Administrators with less than a college education were less likely to say that they gave job descriptions to their employees. On the other hand, priest employees and male religious employees were significantly less likely to say that they had a clear description of their jobs and functions, as were employees with less than a college education. This replicates the findings of Reese (1989:251-4) and Kinsella. (1989:21-22) Table 4 summarizes these findings.

Employees with clear job descriptions were less likely to be thinking of changing their jobs, even though most (75%) felt that they could easily find one. Employees with clear job descriptions felt more secure about their jobs as evidenced by their responses to questions on their long term future with the church and their security if diocesan or parish leadership changed (13a, 13b, and 13c). Employees with clear job descriptions were also more likely to say that they felt part of a vibrant church community.

TABLE 4
% With Job Descriptions

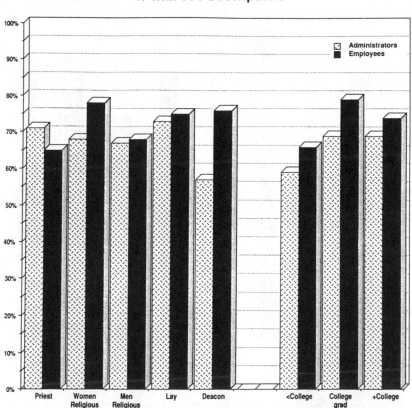

With regard to performance appraisals, there was general agreement between the employees and administrators working in diocesan offices, education and youth/health/charities as to the existence of such appraisals for employees. The practice seems to be more prevalent in youth/health/charities than elsewhere, perhaps because some of these agencies have other, non-church run agencies to serve as reference points. As was the case with job descriptions, however, there was a wide discrepancy between the employees and the administrators (i.e. the pastors) working in parishes on whether or not the employees received performance appraisals. Again, the employees were much less likely to say that they received performance appraisals than the administrators were to say that they gave them. Finally, employees working for religious congregations were more likely to say that they received performance appraisals than the administrators in religious congregations were to admit giving them. This same discrepancy had occurred with regard to job clarity.

TABLE 5
% With Performance Appraisals

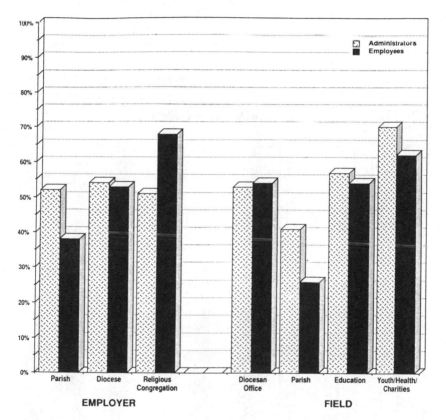

As with job clarity, there was no significant difference between priest, religious and lay *administrators* in their estimation of performance appraisals for employees. Among the *employees,* however, priests were significantly less likely to say they *received* performance appraisals than were the other respondents. This finding supports the work of Reese alluded to above (1989:251-54), that priests are especially underserved by their diocesan supervisors in performance appraisal.

While, among administrators, college and post-college educated respondents were similar in their estimation of employee performance appraisals, among the employees themselves, those with postgraduate work were the least likely to receive such appraisals.

For employees, there was a strong relationship between job clarity and receiving performance appraisals. Those who disagreed with one of these two statements were far more likely to disagree with the other as well. Among those employees who did not consider themselves "Too Old To Change," there was no significant relationship between receiving performance appraisals and whether the respondent was thinking of finding a position outside of the church. No significant relationship existed between any of the job security variables (Q.13) and whether or not an employee had received performance appraisals, nor did a relationship exist between the employee's appraisal of his/her benefits (Q.3) and whether he/she received appraisals. Employees with perfor-

TABLE 6
% With Performance Appraisals

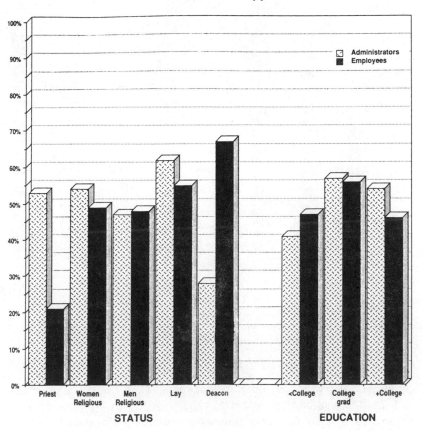

STATUS   EDUCATION

mance appraisals were more likely to feel free to discuss their difficulties with their supervisor (Q. 7d), and to expect always to work for the church.

Most of the relationships described in the preceding paragraph did not apply to administrators, since the wording of their question was different. However, administrators whose offices gave performance appraisals to their employees were more likely to say that employees felt free to discuss difficulties with them.

DISCUSSION

The findings of this study which are most relevant for policy appear to be twofold. First, a vast discrepancy exists between the responses of parish administrators (pastors) and parish employees on whether the employees receive job descriptions and performance appraisals. This discrepancy should be addressed. As Ingram (1980) found in his study of Baptist ministers, pastors may resist providing these safeguards to their employees, but it is vitally necessary that they do so. As will be seen in the following section, it will become more and more difficult to hire and retain qualified personnel at the parish level without them. Secondly, the lack of performance appraisals for priests working in parishes must also be addressed. Reese's (1989:251) criticism that the current appraisal process is perfunctory at best and nonexistent at worst should be considered, and steps taken to remedy the situation. This is especially crucial since, as Scheets (1989a:6) reported, 78% of his priest respondents wished to be promoted on the basis of their ability rather than on seniority.

RECRUITMENT AND RETENTION

THEORETICAL BACKGROUND

A key characteristic of all organizations is that they are particularistic in their hiring practices, even though both bureaucratic efficiency and simple justice would seem to mandate otherwise:

> Particularism means that criteria irrelevant for efficient production (e.g., only relatives of the boss have a chance at top positions), in contrast to universalistic criteria (competence is all that counts) are used to choose employees. The criteria of efficiency and particularism often clash, since the most efficient workers may lack the particular social characteristics desired. For example, few Jews ever rise very high in such industries as steel; few Blacks have thus far been able to break

into many skilled trades in the construction industry. (Perrow, 1986:67)

Since particularistic hiring and promotion criteria may negatively affect the organization's performance (e.g. a Jewish applicant may be the most competent; an executive board composed solely of white males may miss key information well-known to Blacks or females), one might wonder why organizations continue the practice. Perrow suggests (1986:78) that particularistic recruitment and hiring increase the hiring agent's power: since the employee owes his/her job to the good will of the hiring agent rather than to his/her own competence, he or she will be more likely to stay on the agent's "good side" by taking the agent's part in company disputes and power struggles. Restricting recruitment and hiring to applicants of a particular social background also effectively limits the pool of people with whom the applicant must compete, and reserves the better paying, most powerful jobs to the white male elite. (Collins, 1979) Kanter argues (1977:49ff) that particularistic hiring is also a result of the need to trust the occupants of higher-level, more discretionary positions. It is easy to tell immediately if a secretary is typing too slowly or too inaccurately; it is less easy to ascertain if a manager's decision to cut back on a certain research investment was a good or a bad move. In such a situation of uncertainty, the company must simply trust that its managers are making the right decisions. It is easier to trust someone who looks and acts like you:

> At Indsco, the top managers inevitably chose people like themselves in whom to put this trust. The managers spent a lot of time interacting with each other between a third and a half of their time actually in meetings. Interacting with people like oneself is always easier, and there was a decided wish to avoid those with whom communication was felt to be uncomfortable. Deviants and nonconformists were suspect . . . Predictability had the highest value. (Pugh and Hickson, 1989:130)

The result of these pressures was that, despite affirmative action laws, the majority of those recruited for top organizational positions continue to be white, Protestant, and male.

Another concern of business is the retention of its workers and administrators. Americans change jobs quite frequently. One study of managers found that each manager changed positions, on the average, every 3.5 years (Pavalko, 1988:158). Geographic job mobility declines with age, as does interorganizational mobility. After about the age of 40, managers often had pension plans and stock options that made movement outside the organization more costly. Internal movement from one position to another within the company, however, remained high for managers. Unlike management, where upward mobility is possible, occupations with short career ladders have a very high percentage of their occupants completely leaving the field. One North Carolina study found that only 54% of teachers who began teaching in 1974 were still doing so in 1980. Nursing has a similar turnover rate. (Pavalko, 1988:152-54) Turnover among administrators is a problem because upper-level administrators and managers take key knowledge with them when they go. (Perrow, 1986:19) Turnover among lower level employees wastes organizational resources in training new ones, and, with the projected shortage of entry-level employees in the 1990's (Bolick and Nestleroth, 1988:310), there may be fewer new applicants available to train. (There already is a severe nursing shortage, for example.) One of the postulated characteristics of Japanese firms, on the other hand, is lifetime tenure, and several researchers (e.g. Ouchi, 1982) have argued that, if American firms did likewise, there would be more employee loyalty and commitment, less emphasis on short-term and easily measured goals, and more long-range planning and investment.

RECRUITMENT AND RETENTION IN CHURCH ORGANIZATIONS

Priests

The many studies which exist regarding *recruitment* to the priesthood per se are outside the scope of this paper. *Remaining* in the priesthood, however, seems to be directly related to a priest's satisfaction in his work. Schoenherr and Greeley (1975:409) postulated that a priest would continue in his role if he received "a net balance of rewards over costs." (See also Vera, 1982:82) The earlier study found that, while neither the diocese's region of the country nor its centralized or decentralized administrative structure had any impact on a priest's desire to remain a priest, for those priests who valued independent decision-making, a more authoritarian diocesan leadership would lead to withdrawal. (Schoenherr and Greeley, 1975:417-19) In contrast to the pre-1965 period, by the late 1970's, a priest's resignation was more likely to be attributed by his fellow priests to institutional failings rather than to some personal deficiency on the priest's part (Goldner et al, 1977:547). Vera (1982:82) found that priests tended to rate resigned priests as more intelligent and creative than average. According to Schoenherr and Sorrenson's 1982 study, extensive resignations began fairly soon after ordination during the 1965-80 period, and peaked in the second five-year period of ministry. (Schoenherr and Sorenson, 1982:28)

In addition to resignations from the priesthood, there is also the phenomenon of priests leaving parish ministry for other types of service. Little has been done to study this, but La Magdeleine found that it is occurring more frequently. (1986:323) Hall and Schneider's (1973) findings that nonparish jobs have more prestige among priests would appear to provide a motivation for this trend.

Women Religious and Lay Workers

According to Joseph (1982:16), the dominant trend among women religious has been the movement out of school-based education and into new forms of church ministry. If other research is correct, however, this trend may not continue. Wittberg (1989b:15657), for example, found that the women religious working in parishes and dioceses were the most likely to volunteer the information that they planned to leave their jobs in the near future.

Little information exists about the recruitment of lay personnel to church positions. According to Rosenberg and Sullivan (1980:133), approximately 43% of liturgical ministers, 40% of education personnel and 33% of administrative/support personnel had actively sought their positions, while 41%, 42% and 48% of these same categories were recruited or selected by the parish. Another 9% or so in each category "heard about" the opening, and, with another 9%, their job was an outgrowth of some other activity.

Once in their positions, however, lay ministers do not remain long. Fox (1986:165) found that only 11% of the lay ministers she surveyed planned to remain in their present positions for more than four years, despite their former projections, while they were still in training, of a long-term career in parish work. (La Magdeleine, 1986:321) According to Fox (1986:200), the top four reasons for leaving were the desire to do other work, burnout, inadequate salary, and frustration in the work. Burnout was the top-ranked reason cited by the women lay ministers, inadequate salary by the men.

FINDINGS OF THE CURRENT STUDY

Q.7f: The Ability to Hire and Retain Qualified Employees (asked of administrators only)

In general, women were more pessimistic than men about their ability as administrators to hire and retain qualified employees. Similarly, priest administrators were more likely to agree, and lay administrators to disagree, with this question. There was a tendency for greater optimism about the ability to hire and retain employees among the older administrators, as well as among administrators in diocesan offices and for health, youth and charities. Administrators with more than a college education were also more likely to feel able to hire and retain good workers, but there was no significant difference between the responses of administrators working for parishes, dioceses or religious congregations. Table 7 summarizes these findings.

There was also a relationship between the administrators' perceived ability to hire and retain qualified employees and whether they themselves were thinking of changing jobs, as measured by questions 5, 14a, and 14d. Those administrators who perceived themselves as unable to hire or retain good employees were more likely to be thinking of changing jobs themselves.

TABLE 7
% Administrators Able to Hire and Retain Qualified Employees

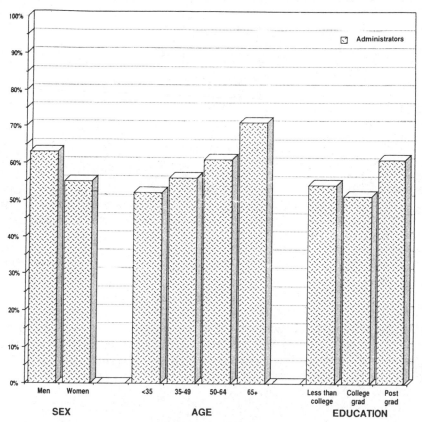

All measures of salary adequacy (Q.2,14b, and 14c) were related to the administrators' perceptions of their ability to hire and retain qualified employees. The more dissatisfied the administrator felt, either with his/her own salary or with the salaries that "church workers" in general received, the more likely he/she was to feel hindered in this regard. Perceived ability to hire and retain qualified employees was similarly related to the administrator's total ranking of the benefits received by

TABLE 7A
% Administrators Able to Hire and Retain Qualified Employees

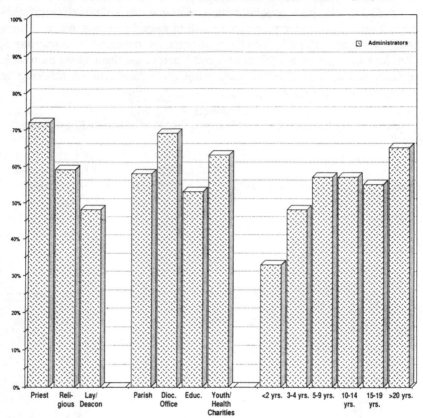

employees. Administrators who thought employees felt insecure (Q.13) were also more likely to complain that they could not hire or retain qualified workers. There was, however, no relationship between an administrator's perception of how easily he/she personally would be able to find another job and his/her perception of ability to hire and retain employees.

Q.14a: Expectation of Always Working for the Church

Overall, a larger percentage of administrators (78%) than of employees (69%) were either very or fairly sure that they would always work for the church. Men were more likely to foresee continued church employment than women, and the likelihood of expecting always to work for the church increased as the respondent grew older. Respondents with some postgraduate training were the most likely to project continued church employment, (perhaps because of the concentration of priests and religious in this category), as were administrators who worked for religious congregations and employees working for parishes. Employees and administrators working in the fields of health, youth and charities were the least likely of all fields to project continued church employment, perhaps because opportunities for similar employment exist under nonchurch auspices. As would be expected, priests were the most likely to anticipate continued church employment, followed by religious. Lay employees and administrators were the least likely to expect always to work for the church. Table 8 summarizes these responses.

For employees, there was the expected strong relationship between anticipated church employment and whether the employee was thinking of changing jobs (Q.S), as well as with the employee's perceived security in his/her job (Q.13a,13b,13c). The tendency for employees insecure in their jobs and for those thinking of changing jobs

TABLE 8
% Expecting Always to Work for Church

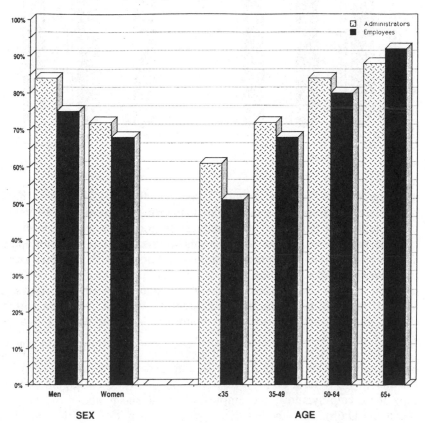

TABLE 8A
% Expecting Always to Work for Church

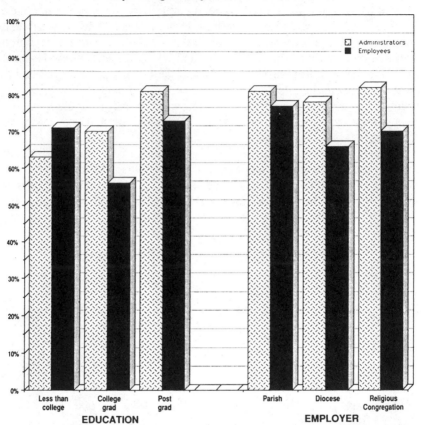

to disagree with Question 14a on continued church employment held true for every one of the demographic categories in questions 15-22.

Employees who rated their salaries as good or excellent with respect to their own or their family needs were more likely to anticipate always working for the church. Employees who rated their salary *comparability* as excellent, however, were less likely to agree with the question than those who rated it "good" or "poor." As Table 9 shows, a summed rating of total benefits (Q.3) together with salary comparability (Q.2c) was consistently related to employees' anticipation of always working for the church.

Other predictable relationships existed between future church employment and the length of time an employee had already worked for the church (long-term employees were more likely to anticipate continuing their employment), the employee's enthusiasm about the church (Q.6a and Q.6b), and whether the employee was put off by the church's

TABLE 8B
% Expecting Always to Work for Church

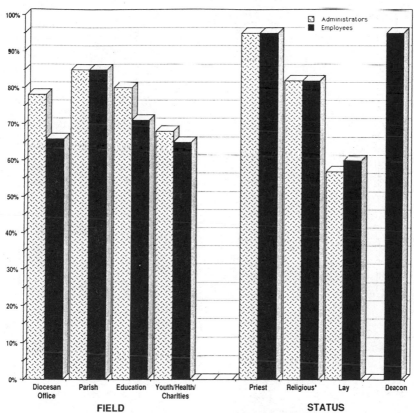

FIELD

STATUS

*82% Religious Administrators and Women Religious Employees
92% Men Religious Employees

restrictive rules (Q.6d). These relationships held true for every demographic category in questions 1522.

Similarly for administrators there was the same strong relationship between expecting always to work for the church and whether the administrator was thinking of changing jobs, how long the administrator had already worked for the church, the administrator's enthusiasm about the church, and whether the administrator was discouraged by the church's restrictive rules. The lay respondents both administrators and employees who felt that the clergy were reluctant to share their duties (Q11e) were much less likely to expect always to work for the church.

For both employees and administrators, there was no relationship between their expectation of continued church employment and how easy they felt it would be for them to change jobs. When this comparison was repeated for the separate demographic categories of questions 1522, no additional relationship was revealed.

TABLE 9
% Expecting Always to Work for the Church (Employees)

RATING OF BENEFITS

DISCUSSION

As the number of priests available for administrative positions within the church declines, and as religious age and retire, the church will hire more lay persons for administrative positions. With this prospective future, however, will come several problems. The youngest age categories of the current administrators, and lay administrators in general, are much more pessimistic about their own ability to hire and retain key employees. This is a probable reflection of the unwillingness of these two groups to remain in church employment themselves. (See Table 8, above) It will be noted that the anticipated retention rate quoted by the young and the lay respondents themselves was approximately equivalent to the retention rates of the teachers and nurses which were cited by Pavalko (1988) as examples of the overly high exit figures for those professions. Several of the actions that could be taken by dioceses to improve their ability to hire and retain key employees would be to increase salary and benefit packages, to address employment security concerns and to work for greater opportunities for women at all levels. The findings on the enthusiasm for church employment of both employees and administrators, and the importance of reducing restrictive rules, may indicate that more cooperative forms of organizational practices could profitably be adopted. Since there is strong resistance in most organizations to debureaucratizing their procedures (e.g. employee participation in decision-making, or small work groups with shared responsibilities), the literature on similar experiments would have to be carefully studied for suggestions on how to proceed. (Zwerdling, 1984)

CONCLUSION

Bureaucratic procedures such as concrete job descriptions and regular performance evaluations are necessary. However, they may sometimes be liabilities. On the one hand, the lack of such procedures, *unless specific cooperative practices are established in their place* (McManus, 1987; Zwerdling, 1984), are quite disempowering for employees. The literature is unanimous, as is the NACPA research, that church workers without job clarity and performance evaluations are dissatisfied and vulnerable. This is especially true in parishes. If pastors continue to be unwilling to provide job descriptions, employment agreements, and performance appraisals to church employees, and if the priests continue to monopolize the top line positions, they may very likely lose the lay employees they already have. (See Fox, 1986:165) On the other hand, the Notre Dame study of parish life (NCCB, 1982) has indicated that more cooperative structures are preferable to a rigid separation of job roles. A balance will have to be achieved between the adoption of sufficiently clear job descriptions and performance evaluations to safeguard the rights of employees, and the collaborative participation of all employees, administrators and non-church employed faithful in the creation of alive and vibrant parish and diocesan structures for the future.

— 3 —

Communications and Grievance Procedures

THEORETICAL BACKGROUND

According to most social theorists, (Perrow, 1986; Weber, 1984) bureaucratic organizations are extremely efficient social mechanisms for harnessing the efforts of many individuals to accomplish a wide variety of tasks, more so than other types of organizations. This, Weber felt, is why organizations rarely discard bureaucratic structures once they have adopted them. Whoever, therefore, controls the policies and activities of a bureaucratic organization is able to influence his/her surroundings to a far greater extent than would be possible for an individual acting alone: not only to dictate the working conditions and financial rewards of hundreds or even thousands of people (although this is certainly done), but also to develop new and lifesaving hospital equipment, to alter the placement of a highway, and even to determine what types of food products will line grocery shelves and what varieties of music and TV programming will fill the airwaves. Critics argue that the enormous power of bureaucratic institutions is often too lightly taken for granted:

> Bureaucracy is a tool, a social tool, that legitimizes control of the many by the few, despite the formal apparatus of democracy, and this control has generated unregulated and unperceived social power. (Perrow, 1986:5) [italics mine]

With such power at issue, it becomes increasingly important to examine both how various groups in an organization exercise their influence, and also the results, in levels of satisfaction or grievance, of the lack of or the misuse of power. A key component in the investigation of these topics is a worker's or an administrator's access to needed information, and his/her ability to structure and summarize such information before it is communicated to others. Whoever determines the channels and content of communication can exercise a great deal of often unperceived influence over the entire institution:

Such mechanisms affect organizational behavior in the following ways: they limit information content and flow, thus controlling the premises available for decisions; they set up expectations so as to highlight some aspects of the situation and play down others; they limit the search for alternatives when problems are confronted, thus ensuring more predictable and consistent solutions; they achieve coordination of effort by selecting certain kinds of work techniques and schedules. (Perrow, 1986:128)

Harrison (1959) gave a good example of the role of information structuring and communication channels in his description of the administrative conference of the American Baptist Church. Even though the American Baptist Convention was hedged about with strict safeguards to insure against its domination by any single group, the agenda setting duties of the administrative staff and their responsibility for the intra Conference communication system subtly influenced the direction and the outcome of all of the Conference deliberations, even when the staff members sincerely attempted to develop more grassroots input. (See also Michels, 1984) More recently, Ammerman (1990) has described the existence of similar agenda setting power in the Southern Baptist Convention. The domination of the SBC's central bureaucracy prior to 1980 by graduates of the moderate seminaries and pastors of the wealthy urban churches was alienating to rural, more conservative members, who felt unable to communicate their priorities for denominational policy. In the resulting battle for control of the denomination's central bureaucracy, the conservatives were helped by the alternative network of communications they had established among themselves. (Ammerman, 1990:171-179) By 1985, the takeover of the Southern Baptist Convention by the conservatives was complete, and the moderate members are now experiencing the same isolation and alienation that the conservatives had before 1980. Who controls, and who is excluded from, the opportunities for communicating input into organizational decision-making is thus vitally important for all groups within the organization. Good communications opportunities are therefore essential for fostering employee satisfaction (Kelly and Harrison, 1990) and for preventing their exit from the organization. (Hirschmann, 1970)

RESEARCH ON COMMUNICATION WITHIN THE CHURCH

Between Priests and Their Supervisors

Access to the communication of information and the ability to communicate one's own information to those in authority are thus ways of defusing dissatisfaction within the church. Through expanding opportunities for "bottom-up" and "top-down" communication, it is possible to increase the feelings of satisfaction which the priests (and the religious and the laity) have, without necessarily diminishing the authority of the bishop and chancery. Reese (1989:64) found that a personal relationship with the bishop was an important determinant of clergy satisfaction: small dioceses had the most satisfied priests. Scheets (1989a:8) found that 70% of the clergy he interviewed wanted the bishop to listen to them more. A positive side effect of the reduction in the number of clergy does seem to be an improvement in priests' satisfaction, since their wishes are now more likely to be taken into consideration. Reese (1989:56) reported that the percentage of priests dissatisfied with the way authority is exercised in the church has decreased from 38% in 1972 to 22% in 1985. "And only 9% of the diocesan priests said that their relationship with their bishop was a problem." (Reese, 1989:56)

Between Religious and Lay Workers and Their Supervisors

Communication, however, is not always as well established between lay or religious employees and their supervisors, especially if the supervisors are ordained clergy. Heslin (1983:165) found that 75% of the sisters she interviewed, who had moved into parish or diocesan ministry from educational administration, complained of a lack of communication and teamwork as indicative of low clergy support. Among the sisters interviewed by Joseph (1982:31), those working within the parishes were the most likely to complain of difficulties with the bureaucratic structure and of general frustration.

According to Rosenberg and Sullivan (1980:93), those women in parish ministry both religious and lay who were substantially more liberal than their pastors were more likely to cite problems with communication and lack of representation in decision making. These problems were cited significantly less often by women whose views were either similar to or more conservative than those of their pastors.

When the parish staff is alienated and dissatisfied, the pastor also experiences strain. Among the Joliet, IL, priests that Fogarty (1988:78-81) studied, "Maintenance of morale among parish staff" was the third most stressful problem stated, and the fourth most frequently experienced. It would seem obvious, therefore, that both administrators and employees could benefit from improved communication procedures.

RESEARCH ON SATISFACTION AND GRIEVANCE PROCEDURES WITHIN THE CHURCH

The level of satisfaction (and the inversely corresponding level of grievance) among those who work for the church is closely related to the issue of what group(s) or individual(s) among them have authority, as well as to the effectiveness of any procedures that the church may devise for rectifying grievances.

Satisfaction and Grievance Among Priests

Many researchers have agreed that authority or lack of authority is the key variable determining the priest's satisfaction and morale:

> One of the most significant findings . . . was the priests' complaint about the exercise of authority in the Church. When they were asked about what was a great personal problem to them, the largest proportion of respondents . . . mentioned "the way authority is exercised in the Church." This reply is noteworthy when we find that they ranked celibacy fifth in a list of fifteen personal problems.
>
> The problem of ecclesiastical mismanagement is not peculiar to the Catholic Church. Laile Bartlett found it in all American denominations and religious organizations. "One of the catchwords around the exits is 'authority.' There's no end of talk about 'due process' and 'top-down decisions', complaints about high-handed orders and rulings of bishops, boards and presbyters." (Fichter, 1988:2356)

Throughout the past two decades, empirical research has confirmed these statements. The priests interviewed by Szafran (1976b) rated their dioceses as more centralized than did the employees of any of the other three organizations studied (the League of Women Voters, a union local, and a bureaucratized delivery company). The priests also thought that decision-making within the church should be less centralized than it was. According to Greeley (1972b:106), 61% of the U.S. priests in 1970 believed that they ought to have a great deal of power in ordering their own lives and in affecting the actions and policies of the church; only 23%, however, thought that they actually did possess such power. The strongest dissatisfaction, Greeley stated, was among the youngest priests. Goldner et al (1977:5436) found that, especially among younger priests, there was increased cynicism and distrust of those in church authority. This was evidenced by the priests' agreement with such statements as "Pastorates have been rewarded on the basis of personal connections" and "The members of the hierarchy don't always believe what they say publicly." (See also Vera, 1982:59 and Dahm, 1981:53) More recently, Reese (1989:52) found that priests still believe their bishops to have more decision-making power than the bishops in fact perceive themselves as having.

Such dissatisfaction with the perceived centralization of authority in the institutional church would seem to mandate the establishment of comprehensive and well developed grievance procedures. Kinsella noted (1989:10) that 68% of the U.S. dioceses and 70% of religious congregations rated themselves as good or excellent in assuring just treatment of their employees' grievances. However, Kinsella also stated (n.d.:3) that he had no figures on how common actual formalized grievance procedures are in U.S. dioceses. For priests, one outlet for grievances over the past two decades has been priests' councils, which, as Kim noted (1979:110), are more likely to have been established in larger dioceses where the clergy have less personal contact with the Bishop. (See also Reese, 1989:64)

According to Goldner (1977:548-49), however, the use of priests' councils often backfires: they may actually elicit hypocrisy in those administrators who are required to justify their actions to the priests. Many of the *real* reasons for actions and policies cannot be stated, due to reasons of confidentiality or incompatibility with the official ideology of the church, (e.g. if Father X is being removed from parish Y to enter an alcohol treatment program, or because the bishop wants to give the position to an old friend.) This made representatives to priests' councils more aware of the political nature of the church and reduced the awe in which leaders were normally held. Another negative effect was found by Hall and Schneider (1972:159), in their observation of the Hartford, CT, Priests' Personnel Board. Since the board's members had often failed in their past dealings with church authorities, they tended to overestimate the likelihood of failing in any given instance. This led to either a passive or an excessively confrontational and suspicious stance, neither of which improved relations between the board and the diocesan hierarchy. Hall and Schneider's study is admittedly old and may be outdated today. Certainly Reese (1989) implies that the shrinking number of active clergy, by giving individual priests more of a voice in their assignments, has reduced this source of tension between the priests and the bishops.

Despite the fact that priests' councils and the other mechanisms to alleviate clergy grievances have not always been effective during the past twenty years, priests have nevertheless continued to press for them, largely because of their self-image as professionals whose interests should be safeguarded vis-a-vis the institution. (Struzzo, 1970; Ference, 1971:515-16; Dahm, 1981:34) Of the priests surveyed in 1970 by Greeley (1972b), 78% supported the establishment of a court of appeals distinct from the hierarchy to guarantee themselves due process of law. Only 58% of the hierarchy saw the need for this. As Ference (1971:515-16) pointed out, priests are uniquely vulnerable as professionals, because their entire legitimacy comes from the organization there are no priests in "private practice." Priests, indeed, have a canonical right to due process, but only the bishop is the judge of what procedures this entails. (Dahm, 1981:11; O'Brien, 1989:10)

Among Religious and Lay Workers

Sisters, too, have attempted to establish various groups to safeguard their rights, but most of these are "unmandated grassroots organizations which lack legitimacy as a bona fide advisory group in the eyes of the hierarchy." (Giniat, 1989:13) Most are either ignored or merely tolerated by the local bishop. The efficacy of the various groups sisters' councils, professional groups, or informal networks which have been formed to represent women religious undoubtedly varies from diocese to diocese. However, Wittberg (1989b) documented the efforts of one diocesan group of pastoral associates to establish a professional organization. The attempt largely floundered because of a lack of diocesan recognition. Few mechanisms exist (other than the religious congregation itself admittedly an often powerful resource) to safeguard the sisters' interests in job disputes. Reese, for example, mentions (1989:266) that the pastor almost always wins in conflicts with DRE's.

Of the lay parish ministers interviewed by Fox (1986:211), 49% (134) said that due process mechanisms were available for their grievances. (22% said such mechanisms were *not* available and 29% did not know.) Kinsella, (n.d.:3) reported that only 46% of the largest parishes in U.S. dioceses had grievance procedures, and it is probable that such practices were even less common in smaller parishes. When asked if they themselves would use due process, 48% of Fox's respondents said yes, 12% said no, and 40% did not know. (Fox, 1986:211) 58% of lay parish ministers knew of colleagues who had lost their jobs in a way that seemed unfair. Of these persons, one-third had gone through grievance procedures; but these procedures had led to a conclusion which was satisfactory to the aggrieved party in only 13% of the cases.

RESULTS OF THE CURRENT STUDY

Q.7c: The Expectation of Just Treatment in Grievance Procedures

Overall, employees and administrators were approximately equally likely to agree with the question on whether just treatment could be expected in grievance procedures, although this is not exactly the same question for each group. The employees' question asked about their *own* expectations of just treatment; the administrators' question asked them whether they thought that *workers* would be treated justly. However, *fewer than half* both of the administrators and the workers (42% and 40%) felt that they could count on just treatment by the church.

For employees, there was no significant relationship between expectation of just treatment and sex, education, length of employment, status as priest/religious/lay, field, or employer. The lack of relationship between expectation of just treatment and the employee's status as priest, religious, or lay held true even when the respondents working in parishes, dioceses and religious congregations were analyzed separately. The only significant relationship was with age: the younger categories of employees were more likely to anticipate that they would not be treated justly.

For administrators, there was no significant relationship between their expectation of just treatment and their education, field, length of employment, and age. However, in contrast to the employees, women administrators were significantly more likely than male administrators to anticipate that their workers would be treated unjustly, and both lay administrators and women religious administrators were also more likely to answer negatively to this question. Administrators working for dioceses and parishes were more likely to say that employees would be treated justly by the church than were administrators working for religious congregations. Table 1 summarizes these differences.

TABLE 1
Expectation of Just Treatment (Administrators % Agreeing)

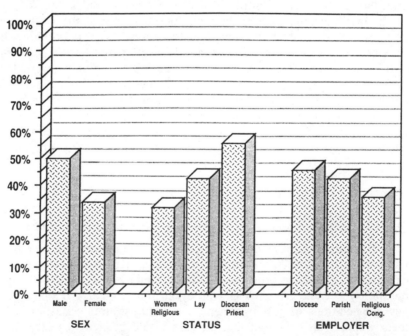

When administrators working in parishes, dioceses and religious congregations were analyzed separately, there was no significant relationship between the expectation of just treatment for workers and the administrator's own status as priest, religious or lay if the respondent worked in a parish. However, in dioceses, both women religious and lay administrators were much less likely, and priests much more likely, to expect just treatment. And in religious congregations, only women religious administrators were more pessimistic in expecting just treatment. A similar relationship to the diocesan pattern appears with question 14d, on whether the respondents were so disturbed by church policies that they were considering leaving church employment. For both employees and administrators, the women religious and the lay workers were more likely to agree with this statement. It seems fairly certain, therefore, that these two groups are significantly more distrustful of the institutional church, especially if they work in diocesan rather than in parish settings.

For both employees and administrators, expectation of just treatment was significantly related to having or giving clear job descriptions and yearly performance appraisals. Employees who had job descriptions and performance appraisals were much more likely to expect just treatment in their grievances, and administrators whose offices provided such services for their employees were also more likely to assume that their workers would be treated justly.

Since communication with one's supervisors has been shown to be such an important determinant of job satisfaction, it is necessary to examine the relationship between expectation of just treatment and the various survey items that measured how well employees communicated with their supervisors and how secure they felt in their jobs. Those employees who participated in decisions about their job (Q.7e), who felt free to discuss difficulties with their supervisors (Q.7d), and who were satisfied with the responsibility they had been given and the recognition they had received for their work (Q. 10b and 10c) were also more likely to expect just treatment from the church. Also, employees who felt that their job was secure even if their supervisor or the parish/diocesan leadership changed were more likely to anticipate being treated justly. There was no relationship between expectation of just treatment by the church and how easy the employees felt it would be to find a job elsewhere.

Similarly, administrators who felt that their employees could discuss job and workplace decisions were more likely to feel that employees could also expect just treatment. Administrators who were satisfied with the responsibility and recognition they themselves received were also more likely to agree that their employees would be treated justly.

Expectation of Just Treatment and Respondents' Feelings About the Church

Several survey items measuring the respondents' feelings about the church (Questions 6a, 6b, 14d, 14e, 11c, 11d, 11e, 11f, 11g, and 11h) were compared to their expectation of just treatment of their grievances.

For both employees and administrators, those who felt part of a thriving church community and those who thought that its current spiritual growth made the present era an exciting period of church history also felt more confident of just treatment by the church. On the other hand, employees and administrators who felt that lay *workers do not* get enough recognition (Q. 11f) or that the clergy are reluctant to share their duties (Q.11e), and those who were not satisfied with the recognition they received for their own work, were less likely to expect just treatment from the church. Employees and administrators who were satisfied with their involvement in ministry and their relations with their coworkers (Q.10a, 10d) were also more likely to anticipate being treated justly.

Looking at some of the measurements of agreement with church teachings on various issues, both employees and administrators who objected to the church's treatment of women (Q.11c) and those who were thinking of leaving their jobs because of church policies (Q.14c) were more likely to doubt that they would receive just treatment. On the other hand, employees and administrators who felt that they must submit to church teachings even if they disagreed (a minority of both groups), and those who expected always to work for the church (Q.14a) even if it meant sacrificing pay and benefits (Q.14b) were more likely to believe that the church would treat them justly. Both males and females, when analyzed separately, showed a strong relationship between their expectation of just treatment and their opinions on the church's treatment of women.

Expectation of Just Treatment and Overall Church Dissatisfaction

In order to determine which of the survey items listed in the preceding section might be combined to form a scale indicating dissatisfaction with the church's teachings and/or employment practices, a factor analysis (Principal Components, Varimax Rotation) was performed on these items. This procedure indicated that the employees' and the administrators' answers to questions 11c (the church's treatment of women), 11e (clergy perceived as reluctant to share duties), 11f (lay workers not given enough recognition), 14d (church policies may cause respondent to stop working for it), 14e (always submitting to church teaching reverse coded), and 6d (restrictive church rules) varied together and could be combined into a "General Dissatisfaction Scale." Low scores on this scale would indicate satisfaction with and high scores dissatisfaction with church policies. The resulting scales ranged from 3 to 30, with an average of 16 for employees and 17 for administrators. Both were significantly related to expectation of just treatment.

For both employees and administrators, women religious were the most likely to be dissatisfied; priests, deacons and male religious were the least likely. Employees and administrators working for religious congregations also scored higher in dissatisfaction than workers for par-

TABLE 2
Most Dissatisfied Groups (% Dissatisfied)

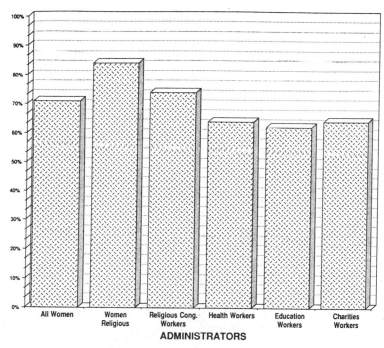

ADMINISTRATORS

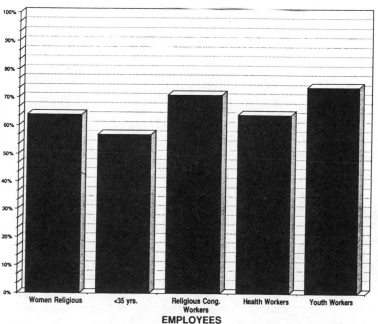

EMPLOYEES

TABLE 2A
Least Dissatisfied Groups (% Dissatisfied)

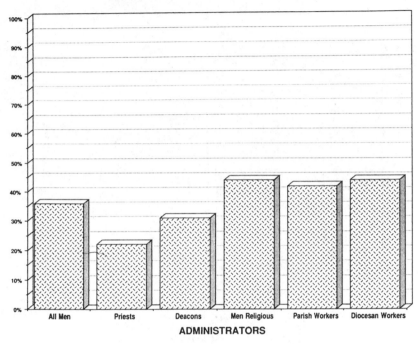

ADMINISTRATORS

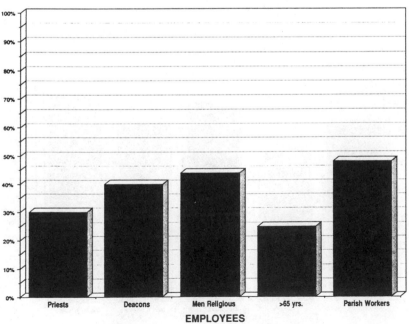

EMPLOYEES

ishes and dioceses. It should be noted that the scale measured dissatisfaction with *church* policies, NOT the *employer's* policies, and so it
cannot be assumed that those who work for religious congregations are
dissatisfied with the policies of their employing institution.

Table 2 summarizes these differences.

Health administrators and employees were more dissatisfied, as
were youth ministry employees and educational and charities administrators. Employees and administrators working in parishes were the
least dissatisfied. No clear relationship appeared between length of
employment and dissatisfaction, nor between having a clear job description and dissatisfaction. Although there was a significant relationship
between sex and dissatisfaction for administrators (with women administrators much more dissatisfied than men), this relationship did not
exist for employees. And, finally, there was a significant relationship
between age and dissatisfaction for employees (the younger age categories of employees were more dissatisfied than the older ones), but this
relationship did not exist for the administrators.

Communication and Worker Satisfaction

Previous literature appears to indicate that opportunities for
employees to communicate their concerns to their supervisors and to
participate in decisions about their work are important ways to reduce
their dissatisfaction. Two questions (7d and 7e) on the NACPA survey
measure whether employees felt free to discuss job difficulties and to
participate in workplace decisions. Overall, administrators were more
likely (82%) to say that their employees felt free to discuss difficulties
with them than the employees were (73%) to agree that they indeed felt
free to do so. There was no significant difference between the responses
of priest, religious and lay *administrators* concerning how free their
employees felt to discuss difficulties. Among *employees,* however,
women religious felt significantly more free to discuss with their supervisors, and priests felt significantly less free to do so. The percentages
for male religious and deacons are distorted by the low numbers of respondents.

The more free employees felt to discuss their difficulties, and the
more they participated in decisions about their jobs, the more satisfied
they expressed themselves with their ministry and the recognition and
responsibility they received in it. (Q. 10a, 10b, 10c) Similarly,
employees who felt free to discuss difficulties and participate in decisions were more likely to feel secure about their jobs. (Q. 13a, 13b,
13c), more likely to anticipate always working for the church (Q.14a),
and less likely to be thinking of changing their jobs (Q.S). Those
employees who scored high on the discussion and participation questions were less dissatisfied when measured on the dissatisfaction scale

developed in the preceding section of this report, as well as when measured on the individual items that made up this scale.

DISCUSSION

The results of the present study support previous findings that open lines of communication with one's supervisors and the ability to participate in decisions about the workplace are two important factors in reducing dissatisfaction among employees. For women religious administrators, there also appears to be a consistent pattern of dissatisfaction and distrust of the church as employer, whether this is measured by the question on just treatment or by the overall dissatisfaction scale. Even though the women religious *employees* are significantly more likely than most respondents to say they felt free to discuss their difficulties with their supervisors, and even though there was no difference between women religious employees and the other employees in their expectation of just treatment, women religious administrators were singularly disenchanted when compared to their nonadministrative fellow religious. If Heslin (1983), Joseph (1982), Wittberg (1989c), and Rosenberg and Sullivan (1980) are correct, there may be something uniquely difficult about ceasing to work for their own congregational sponsored institutions and working for the institutional church that brings about this attitude change in women religious administrators.

CONCLUSION

The overall low level (40%) of expectation of just treatment by the church, the consistently higher levels of dissatisfaction among women religious administrators and employees under 35, and the lack of freedom felt by priest employees to discuss their differences with their supervisors, all pose challenges for the institutional church in the years to come. Perhaps the greater satisfaction with job descriptions and performance appraisals felt by the women religious and lay employees or administrators working for religious congregations could indicate that structures there are more empowering and could serve as a model to reduce tensions among employees and administrators working elsewhere in the church.

— 4 —

Pay and Benefits

THEORY AND COMPARATIVE RESEARCH

Workers in the various jobs that are available in twentieth century capitalist societies differ widely in the pay and benefits which they earn. For example, income varies by region in the United States. To some extent, this merely reflects the higher cost of living in these regions: the median income in the Northeast was $28,069 in 1987, but the Consumer Price Index there was also the highest in the country. (121.8) The next highest region was the West (median income $27,914; CPI 119.0), followed by the Midwest (median income $25,772; CPI 116.1), and the South (median income $23,719; CPI 116.4). (Statistical Abstract of the United States, 1990:445)

Another way of looking at inequalities in earnings is by household. In 1987, the median income of male-headed, single-earner households was $31,534; dual earner households averaged $34,782. In contrast, households headed by divorced women averaged $17,597 in income, and never-married women (with or without children) earned $15,759. (Statistical Abstract of the United States, 1990:445)

Sociologists have advanced two theories for discrepancies in salary among workers. The older theory first argued by Davis and Moore in the 1940's holds that those jobs which require a large personal investment of time and effort to learn and practice (e.g. brain surgery), or which require a level of intelligence and/or skill not widely distributed among the general population (e.g. computer designer, professional athlete), or which expose the worker to significant hazards (e.g. cleaning up Three Mile Island) must offer correspondingly higher remuneration and benefits in order to provide sufficient incentives for workers to fill them. (Davis and Moore, 1945) Critics, however, have since pointed out that salaries and benefits do not always correspond to the qualifications required for a given job. For example, a 1983 study of public sector jobs in the state of Washington (mandated by a 1978 lawsuit) found that occupations which required similar levels of skill paid widely different salaries: warehouse worker ($17,030) vs. laundry worker ($12,276); chemist ($25,625) vs. registered nurse ($20,952); computer systems analyst ($25,920) vs. librarian ($21,969). (Hodson and Sullivan, 1990:140)

These critics have advanced a second theory, which holds that the chief determinant of wages and benefits in a particular occupation is the degree to which that occupation is the protected preserve of the white male elite, whether as professional and managerial jobs protected by informal mentoring and "weak tie" contacts, or as craft and industrial jobs protected by skilled trade unions. (See Granovetter, 1973; and McPherson and SmithLovin, 1984). Women and members of racial and/or ethnic minorities, excluded from these positions, must compete for the limited number of remaining jobs, which depresses the salaries these latter jobs may command. The oversupply of workers keeps the salaries for "ghettoized" occupations such as secretary (99% female), textile factory worker (78% female; 40% Black or Hispanic), and social worker (66% female; 25% Black or Hispanic) disproportionately low when compared to occupations requiring similar skills which are held by white males. (Hodson and Sullivan, 1990:132133) Women's earnings as a percentage of men's have remained constant within 6 percentage points for over 20 years: 64% in 1955, 60% in 1965, 59% in 1975, and 65% in 1987. (Hodson and Sullivan, 1990:139) In 1964, Blacks earned, on average, 50% of what whites did. This ratio climbed to a high of 62% in 1975, and has since fallen to 56% in 1987, the most recent year for which figures are available. (Hodson and Sullivan, 1990:137)

PAY AND BENEFITS IN CHURCH OCCUPATIONS

Priests and Ministers

Although the official annual salary of Catholic priests averages about $7,000, the addition of housing, stipends and benefits raises the total equivalent compensation a priest receives to $29,700 in 1988 dollars. (Hoge, Carroll and Scheets, 1988:35) As Table 1 shows, however,

TABLE 1
Average Annual Salaries and Benefits: Priests and Ministers

	Catholic Priests	Episcopalians Priests	Lutheran Ministers	Methodist Ministers
U.S. Average	$26,184	$41,029	$39,059	$35,308
Western Region	30,662	40,524	38,055	37,790
Northeast	26,070	46,501	35,534	20,295
Southeast	23,681	40,424	27,051	20,851

Source: Hoge, Carroll, Scheets, p. 150-51

this is still far below what ministers earn in the Episcopalian, Methodist and Lutheran churches.

It is difficult, of course, to know how to compare these figures. The priests' total compensation is almost exactly at the U.S. median for 1987 ($25,986). The figures for married Protestant ministers should more fittingly be compared to the median salary for male household heads ($31,584). Rather than comparing their total remuneration to the national average, however, priests are more likely to compare their base salaries to those of their Protestant counterparts, and may feel undercompensated as a result.

Benefits for clergy present a more mixed picture. According to Kinsella (1989:25), and Hoge, Carroll and Scheets(1988:52, 152), 98% of Catholic dioceses provide retirement benefits and health insurance for priests, 100% provide education allowances, and 85% travel allowances. In addition to these benefits, many Protestant ministers also received Social Security and Workers Compensation reimbursements. (Hoge, Carroll and Scheets, 1988:52) Table 2 shows the level of various benefits for the clergy from four denominations.

TABLE 2
Benefit Levels: Priests and Ministers

	Catholic Priests	Episcopalians Priests	Lutheran Ministers	Methodist Ministers
Health	$1,381	$2,824	$1,649	$1,444
Retirement	999	4,609	3,229	2,662
Travel	3,121	2,932	3,000	2,822
Education	531	598	594	473
Social Security & Workers Comp.		1,799*	1,872*	1,181*

*For those who receive this: 36% Episcopalians, 8% Methodists, 47% Lutherans / Source: Hoge, Carroll, Scheets, p. 150-51

Women Religious

The undercompensation of women religious in the Catholic Church, extending over decades, was brought to the attention of the American public by the Wall Street Journal in 1986. (May 19, p.1) According to the most recent figures published by the TriConference Retirement project and the National Association of Treasurers of Religious Institutes, only four of the 132 arch/dioceses responding to a 1989 survey paid religious a lay equivalent salary. The modal response (40 of the 132 dioceses) was that religious were paid between $10,000 and $12,000. As with the priests, the official salary figures must be considered in the light of the other benefits which religious receive: 118 of the 132 dioceses provided health benefits in addition to the base salaries (the median coverage specified was between $1,000 and $1,500 per year); 113 provided additional retirement benefits (median approximately $1,000); 53 provided housing; 58 furnished a living allowance; 114 either provided a car or paid for ministry travel expenses. About 30 dioceses reported providing other benefits, some of which included educational stipends, life insurance, time away for retreat or vacation, dental insurance, and bonuses for above-average work loads. When these benefits are included, the total remuneration of religious is raised substantially, although probably not to the level of the priests' compensation. The Hoge, Carroll and Scheets study (1988) sampled only 25 sisters among full-time parish workers, and they cautioned that their figures might not be representative. According to their study, however, these sisters averaged only $15,120 in total salary and benefits, as compared to the $29,700 for priests.

Lay Workers

According to Rosenberg and Sullivan (1980:59), only 8% of all women parish ministers in the Catholic Church were paid at all in 1980, and of those who were paid, only 12% earned more than $10,000 per year. Fox's (1986) study found only 17 respondents out of the 183 full-time paid lay workers she interviewed were paid more than $21,000 per year in 1985. Those respondents who planned to leave church employment within six years were more than twice as likely to say that their salary was unfair. (Fox, 1986:195) The Hoge, Carroll and Scheets study (1988) found that full-time lay professional ministers in the Catholic church had an average salary that was somewhat higher ($19,818) than the average salary of women religious ($15,120), but still far lower than the U.S. median of $25,896. Table 3 summarizes the differences in lay salaries across denominations.

Hoge, Carroll and Scheets further break these figures down by type of parish ministry and by region, but these figures are not reproduced here. (1988:162-179)

FINDINGS OF THE CURRENT STUDY

Q.2: Rating of Salary Adequacy (Employees Only)

The employees' rating of their salary adequacy was significantly related to their answers on several others of the survey questions. With regard to status, single parents and married respondents without children were the most likely to rate their salaries as fair or poor. Married respondents with children were less likely to say this. In responding to the question on salary comparability (Q.2c), diocesan priests are obviously aware that their salaries are not comparable to ministerial salaries elsewhere. Since diocesan priests considered their salaries to be only the official monetary part and not the in-kind subsidies they also receive (Hoge, Carroll, Scheets, 1988:35), their feelings of relative deprivation are doubtless more severe than they otherwise would be.

TABLE 3
Lay Salaries and Benefits

	Catholic	Episcopalian	Lutheran	Methodist
Salary	$19,818	$16,754	$19,463	$23,147
Health	1,255	1,984	1,005	1,089
Retirement	958	1,457	1,805	1,363
Travel	710	1,256	1,563	521
Education	495	348	487	461

Source: Hoge, Carroll, Scheets, p. 162

Women employees were more likely to rate their salaries as fair or poor than men employees were. Less educated employees were also more likely to rate their salaries as fair or poor. No significant relationship appeared between the employees' rating of their salaries and whether they were employed by a parish, a diocese, or a religious congregation.

For those employees who were the sole wage earners in their families, respondents with smaller reported salaries were more likely to rate their salaries as inadequate. The relationship between family income and perceived salary adequacy was not significant if the employee was not the sole wage earner in the family.

Employees' rating of their salary adequacy was also significantly related to.

1. whether the employee was thinking of finding a position elsewhere. (Those who rated their salaries fair or poor were more likely to be thinking of change.)

2. whether the employee thought he/she could easily find another job. (Those who thought that they could were more dissatisfied with their salaries.)

3. whether the employee thought that he/she might some day be unable to afford to work for the church. (Those dissatisfied with their salaries were more likely to agree with this question, and

4. whether the employee was willing to make financial sacrifices in order to work for the church. (Those who rated their

salaries as "good" or "excellent" were more likely to say they were willing to make financial sacrifices.)

Administrators and Employees Compared

Most of the salary questions on the administrators' questionnaire measured what they thought about their *employees'* salaries, and thus could not be analyzed as the employees' responses had been in the preceding section. However, the administrators *did* report their *own* family income, and, for those administrators who were the sole source of that income, it can be assumed that this reported family income represented their salaries from church service. The two groups can thus be compared on this variable.

For administrators, there was a significant relationship between the amount of income they reported and whether they were thinking of changing their jobs (Q.5) or whether they expected always to work for the church (Q.14a). Interestingly, however, those administrators who earned more money were the most likely to be thinking of looking for a job elsewhere. For employees, there was a barely significant relationship between expecting always to work for the church and income, but not for thinking of changing jobs. Administrators who made less money were more likely to say that they were willing to sacrifice pay and benefits to continue church employment (Q.14b), possibly because these administrators were disproportionately likely to be priests or religious. The opposite was true for employees.

On the other hand, among employees who were the sole earners of the income reported in Q.24, there was a significant relationship between their income and how likely they were to say that financial pressures would cause them to stop working for the church (Q.14c), and with how satisfied they were with the recognition they received for their work (Q.10c). Lay administrators' responses did not show a significant relationship between income and these two questions. Both employees and administrators who earned lower salaries were more likely to say that the laity expected religious and priests to work long hours for little money (Q. 11g). There was no significant relationship between reported income and perceived ease of finding other employment (Q.4), or between income and satisfaction with ministerial responsibility (Q.10a and 10b) and church policies (Q.14d).

The telephone survey of Catholics who did not work for the church showed that only 15.3% felt that the amount of money lay church workers received to meet their family needs was "good" or "excellent" (67.1% felt that it was "fair" or "poor"). (Q.2b) On the average, only one third of the telephone respondents rated the various benefits provided to church workers as "excellent" or "good" (Q.7) and 60.4% assumed that church workers accepted these low benefits and pay as part of their job (Q.1d), rather than because they simply couldn't get as good a job elsewhere (Q.lb). Only 17.6% thought that this latter statement was true. And 46% thought that people who work for the church were never fired (Q.lf). Table 4 summarizes the estimates which the telephone respondents gave for the salaries in various types of paid church positions.

TABLE 4
Estimates of Salaries of Various Church Positions (percent)

	Less Than $10,000	$10,000- $19,999	$20,000- $29,999	Greater than $30,000	Don't Know	Mean
Priests	10.5	19.4	19.6	13.8	36.3	$19,232
Sisters	18.5	27.3	12.4	2.5	38.0	13,076
Brothers	17.0	25.8	12.6	1.3	41.9	13,036
DRE's	10.9	25.7	15.9	7.2	38.6	16,643
Lay School Teachers	4.6	37.0	19.9	2.2	35.5	16,506
Secretaries	14.4	40.1	8.1	0.6	36.6	13,072
Janitors	16.4	39.5	5.8	0.9	36.9	12,474
Catholic Charities*	15.7	21.0	4.6	0.6	42.1	11,154

*16.0% said $0 or voluntary

JOB SECURITY OF EMPLOYEES

Q.13d and 13e: Illness and Retirement Benefits

When the employees' ratings of their benefits (Q.3) were added together to form a variable measuring their evaluation of their total benefits package, the resulting variable was significantly related to how secure employees felt about their retirement and health provisions. Employees who felt that their retirement and long-term future were secure were also more likely to expect always to work for the church, and less likely to be thinking of changing their jobs. The employees who had been working a long time for the church were the most likely to feel secure. Single, single parent and married employees were less likely to feel secure about their retirement and health provisions than were priests and religious. Among diocesan priests, deacons and religious, there was no significant relationship between their security in illness and whether they worked for parishes, dioceses, or religious congregations; for lay employees, however, those working for parishes were significantly less likely to feel secure about their health benefits.

Priests working for parishes were less likely to say their retirement was secure than were priests working for the diocese.

Q.13a, 13b, 13c: In Times of Leadership Change

Employees who felt secure if their supervisor or the diocesan leadership changed were more likely to expect always to work for the church, and less likely to be thinking of changing their jobs. However, there was no relationship between length of employment and how secure the employee felt. There was also no significant relationship between the security variables and whether or not an employee thought it would be easy to find another job.

DISCUSSION

The most striking finding to emerge from this section is how much the church depends upon its religious and diocesan priest employees. They work for below average pay in top administrative jobs which would otherwise command a salary that would be much higher, and they are significantly more likely than lay workers to feel secure in

TABLE 5
Rating of Benefits of Church Workers as "Fair" or "Poor" by Catholic Laity

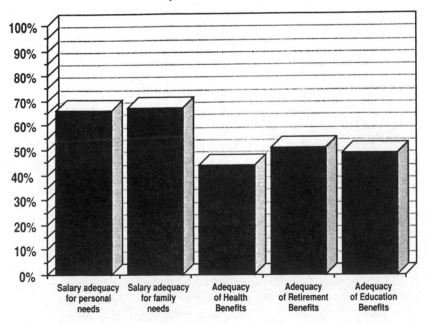

their employment and to expect always to work for the church. In the near future, however, most religious and many priests will reach the age when they will need to retire. It will be difficult to attract lay employees to take their place, especially in the Eastern and far Western states, where the discrepancy between lay salaries in church employment and the cost of living is quite large. Most church lay workers will continue to have to rely on secondary sources of income, whether earned by themselves in second jobs or by their spouses. This is hardly an attractive situation to potential employees. The NACPA survey of Catholics not working for the church shows that, even though 90% would be happy if a close relative chose to work for the church, they did not rate highly the pay (Q. 1, 2, and 6) and benefits (Q.7) which church workers receive, and 60% believed that church workers view low pay as part of the job. Also, 70% of the respondents did not think lay workers get enough recognition for their work (Q.4).

The percentages of the laity who think church workers should have opportunities for sabbaticals (85.4%), continuing education opportunities (96.3%), and promotion (97.4%) are also quite high.

CONCLUSION

The declining numbers of priests and religious in church positions and the expectations for pay and benefits for church workers are two factors influencing job satisfaction for church workers The data in the NACPA survey indicate a probable level of personal expectations that church employment would not currently be able to meet. Recent research by Greeley and McManus (1987) shows that the contributions upon which the church will have to rely in order to meet increased lay expectations for pay and benefits have actually declined by 50% in recent years Filling organizational positions with more highly paid employees in a time of decreasing funds will pose a severe challenge to the church in the coming decades.

— 5 —

Affirmative Action

The topic of Affirmative Action, especially for women, has been an essential part of all the subject matter discussed so far. It would be impossible to address adequately the issue of promotion without mentioning the differential expectations men and women have of promotion opportunities, or the topic of grievances without noting that the women administrators among the respondents were more dissatisfied than the men, or the topic of salary and benefits without pointing out that women still earn less than men in most occupations, church-related occupations included. It was essential, therefore, to cover these issues as they arose. However, for many readers, the dispersal of the findings on Affirmative Action throughout the body of the report may obscure the underlying patterns evident in the issue. Therefore, it was deemed necessary to devote a fifth area to the issue of Affirmative Action considered separately. The first section of this report, therefore, will summarize the theories and research which was covered in the other areas. A subsequent section will detail additional findings related to Affirmative Action.

THEORY

As was pointed out earlier, social theorists give several reasons why organizations or individuals might discriminate against women or minorities in their hiring and promotion practices. Collins (1979) noted that restricting entrance to the higher-paying positions to white males reduces the competition for these positions, while simultaneously increasing the competition for (and thus lowering the wages of) lower-level jobs. Perrow (1986) held that hiring and promoting on bases other than competence increased the power base of the hiring agent, for those hired would be conscious that they owed their positions to the agent's favor. And Kanter (1977) pointed out that upper level managers find it easier to trust colleagues who are like themselves.

For whichever reason, a dual labor market exists (Braverman, 1974; Glenn and Feldberg, 1977; Galle et al, 1985), in which women and minorities are disproportionately concentrated in low-paying jobs with short or nonexistent promotion ladders. Women's earnings have varied during the past three decades, but have remained at between 59% and 65% of the earnings of men. Blacks earned 50% of the salaries of whites in 1964, 62% in 1975, and 56% in 1987. (Hodson and Sullivan, 1990:137-39) A "glass ceiling" limits promotion opportunities: a recent study by Korn/Ferry International, a recruiting firm, and the Anderson Graduate School of Management at UCLA has found that, among 698 top executives surveyed at 1000 companies, only 3% were women and 1% were Black, Asian or Latino. This is only a slight improvement from 1979, when the figures were 1% and 0.4%, respectively. ("Ten Years Later," 1990:52) Women and minorities are usually shunted into staff rather than line positions, and fill a "women's slot" or a "black slot" from which there is no further advancement. Even though women are more likely than men to value opportunities to learn new skills (Hay Group, III4), their jobs are disproportionately "degraded and deskilled." (Glenn and Feldberg, 1977. See also Garson, 1988)

PREVIOUS RESEARCH ON AFFIRMATIVE ACTION AND THE CHURCH

According to research done by *Conscience*, (Nov/Dec. 1988), priests hold 64% of the top 19 diocesan-level positions in the Catholic Church. Lay men hold 18% of these positions, mostly in finance and administration. Women (religious and lay together) hold only 16%, concentrated in the stereotypically "female" areas of schools and religious education. Only 9% of the finance directors, 12% of the chancellors, and 2% of the tribunal judges were women. On the other hand, 52% of superintendents of schools were women (45% sisters and 7% lay), as were 59% of the diocesan directors of catechesis (48% sisters and 11% lay) and 34% of diocesan directors of worship (18% sisters, 16% lay). Of a total of 5492 positions filled in 175 dioceses, 84% were filled by men and 16% by women. (Conscience, 1988:314) Similar research has not been done for the proportion of diocesan positions which are filled by members of ethnic minorities, persons with disabilities, or those over 50 years of age.

The little evidence available indicates that women in church employment are less well paid than men are. Of the lay parish ministers interviewed by Fox (1986:1756), 80 of the 133 women (60%) earned less than $15,000 a year, whereas only 10 of the 49 men (20%) did. The Hoge, Carroll and Scheets study (1988) found that sisters in parish ministry earned an average of $15,120 in pay and benefits, as compared to $29,700 for priests.

Research by La Magdeleine (1986:323), Rosenberg and Sullivan (1980:75) and Heslin (1983) found that women and lay workers in general were disproportionately concentrated in dead-end staff positions within the church, rather than in line positions with greater possibility for advancement. Heslin's (1983:115) and Wittberg's (1989b:1567) research indicated that the occupants of these positions were more dissatisfied and more likely to anticipate leaving their jobs. Similar patterns were discovered by Carroll (1982:129) among women ministers in Protestant churches.

THE FINDINGS OF THE NACPA RESEARCH

Women

The current research also uncovered significant discrepancies between the responses of the men and women surveyed. Women employees and administrators were more likely than men to value promotion opportunities, and women administrators were more dissatisfied with the promotion opportunities provided by the church. Among both employees and administrators, women were more likely than men to rate the church as fair or poor at hiring and promoting women. (Q.8a, 9a) Women were also more likely to value educational opportunities and sabbaticals, and women administrators were more dissatisfied with the educational opportunities provided them by the church.

Women employees and administrators were also more likely than men to rate their current salaries as fair or poor, and they also consistently ranked their benefits lower than did the male respondents. (Q.3) Women employees and administrators were less likely to say they felt secure about their long-term future with the church, or about what would happen to them if their supervisor changed, or if they retired or became incapacitated. (Q.13) The women were more likely than the men to say that financial constraints might some day cause them to quit church employment. (Q.14c)

As might be expected, therefore, the women respondents, and especially the women administrators, were more dissatisfied with the church employment. Women administrators (but not women employees) were more likely than men to anticipate being treated unjustly in disputes with the church, and women administrators scored higher than men administrators on the overall dissatisfaction index. The women administrators were more pessimistic than the men about their ability to hire and retain qualified employees. (Q.7f) Among both employees and administrators, the women respondents were more likely than the men to object to the church's treatment of women and to say that the clergy were reluctant to share their duties. (Qs. 11c and 11e) Women administrators were less likely to feel part of a thriving church community than the men administrators were, (Q.6a) and more likely to agree that church workers were discouraged by restrictive church rules. (Q.6d)

This dissatisfaction is likely to result in a greater turnover rate among women working for the church. Among both employees and administrators, women were less likely than men to foresee continued church employment, and more likely to have thought of changing their jobs. (Qs. 5, 14a) The women respondents were also more likely to say that, unless the church became more open in some of its policies, they might cease working within it. (Q. 14d)

Findings on Other Groups

The NACPA questionnaire did not include items on the race or disability status of the respondents. Age, however, was asked, but the patterns of the responses were less clear. There was no significant difference between the various age categories of the respondents in their satisfaction, either with the educational or the promotional opportunities offered by the church. Younger respondents (those under 35) were, however, significantly more likely to value promotion opportunities, were less likely to expect just treatment from the church, and were more likely to score high on the overall dissatisfaction scale.

ADDITIONAL RESULTS OF THE CURRENT RESEARCH

There was no significant difference between males and females, among either employees or administrators, in how easily they thought they would be able to find a position elsewhere. This relationship also held true for each educational level when considered separately. Initially, it was thought that this finding might be distorted by the responses of the priests and women religious. But, when only the lay employees and the lay administrators were considered, the results were equally ambiguous. Lay administrators still showed no significant variation by sex in how easily they thought they would be able to find alternative employment. Among the employees, women were more likely either to say that they could easily find another position or else to be unsure whether or not they could do so.

Q.8b and 8c: Rating the Church's Record in Recruiting and Promoting Blacks and Other Minorities

For both employees and administrators, there was a statistically significant relationship between the amount of education a respondent had and how likely he/she was to say that the church had a good record in hiring Blacks. (Those with more education were more likely to rate the church as fair or poor.) The same relationship also held true for administrators in their estimation of the church's record in hiring other minorities and in promoting Blacks, but, for employees, there was no significant relationship between education and these variables.

There was no relationship for either administrators or employees between the length of their own employment and their estimation of the church's record in hiring Blacks. However, administrators employed between five and fourteen years were more likely to rate the church's record in promoting Blacks more favorably than either longterm or recently hired administrators. The relationship between education and the respondents' rating of church hiring and promoting other minorities was not significant.

There was a strong and significant relationship for both employees and administrators between the dissatisfaction variable and their rating of the church's efforts to hire and promote Blacks and other minorities. Similarly strong relationships held between each of the component variables of the dissatisfaction scale and employees' and administrators' rating of the church in hiring and promoting Blacks and other minorities. Finally, other questions that indicate suspicion of or dissatisfaction with the church (Q.7c on confidence of just treatment of grievances, for example, and Q. 11h acceptance of sisters in nontraditional positions) were similarly related to the respondents' rating of the church's record. In other words, the more dissatisfied an employee or an administrator was with other aspects of church practice, the more likely he/she was to be critical of the church's affirmative action record.

There was also at times a relationship between a respondent's satisfaction with his/her ministry, responsibility and recognition (Qs. 10a, 10b, and 10c) and respondents' rating of the church's record in hiring and promoting Blacks and other minorities. Both employees and administrators who were satisfied with the amount of recognition they received for their work were also more likely to approve of the church's affirmative action stance. Employees who were satisfied with the amount of responsibility they had been given were more likely to rate the church highly in promoting Blacks and other minorities; administrators were more likely to rate the church highly in hiring and promoting Blacks. Employees who were satisfied with their ministerial involvement were more likely to approve of the church's record in hiring and promoting Blacks and in promoting other minorities; none of these relationships were significant for administrators. In other words, the dissatisfaction variables were more consistent predictors than the satisfaction variables of an employee's or an administrator's evaluation of the church's record in hiring and promoting Blacks and other minorities.

Q.8d, 8e, 8f: Rating the Church's Record in Hiring and Promoting Persons with Disabilities, the Old and the Young

With regard to the dissatisfaction variable and its components, an identical relationship occurred with respondents' evaluation of the church's record in hiring and promoting persons with disabilities, the old and the young as was reported in the previous section with regard to the hiring and promotion of Blacks and other minorities. General dissatisfaction with the church, therefore, seems to be an extremely accurate predictor of whether an employee or an administrator will rate the church well or poorly in the affirmative action variables.

With regard to education, employees with more education were more likely to disapprove of the church's record in hiring persons with disabilities; administrators with more education were more likely to disapprove of the church's record both in hiring and promoting this group. No significant relationship existed, either for employees or administrators, between amount of education and their rating of the church in hiring and promoting the old or the young. Similarly, no significant relationship existed between length of employment and these variables, with the one exception that employees who had worked longer for the church were more likely to rate the church highly in promoting older workers.

Employees who were satisfied with the recognition, responsibility and ministerial involvement they experienced were also more likely to rate the church highly in hiring and promoting persons with disabilities. Administrators who ranked high on these satisfaction variables were more likely to approve of the church's record in promoting, but not in hiring, persons with disabilities. Employees who were satisfied were also more likely to approve of the church's record in hiring those over 50; the relationship for administrators was not significant. With regard to hiring young workers, employees and administrators who were satisfied with their recognition and ministerial involvement were more likely to rate the church highly; the relationship between satisfaction with responsibility and hiring young workers held true for employees only.

It is more than possible that the respondents, particularly the employees, simply did not know enough about the church's affirmative action record with regard to these groups to have an informed opinion. If this were the case, they would simply tend to answer Qs.8 and 9 on the church's affirmative action record according to their predispositions of general overall satisfaction or dissatisfaction with the church.

Q.8a: Rating the Church's Record in Hiring and Promoting Women

Exactly the same relationship occurred for employees and administrators between the dissatisfaction variables and their estimation of the church's record in hiring and promoting women as has been reported in the two preceding sections. The relationship with the satisfaction variables was strong, too. In general, employees and administrators who were satisfied with the responsibility, ministerial involvement and recognition they had received were more likely to rate the church highly in hiring and promoting women. No relationship existed, however, between the amount of education a respondent had received and his/her estimation of the church's affirmative action record with regard to women. This finding can be interpreted, perhaps, to indicate that the church's record with regard to women is more well-known than its record with regard to the other groups, and thus a respondent did not need more education in order to be aware of it. When length of employment was considered, those employees and administrators working between five and nineteen years were the most negative.*

DISCUSSION AND CONCLUSION

The evidence reported strongly supports the contention that women who work for the church (especially the women administrators) were more dissatisfied with their promotional and educational opportunities, their salaries and benefits, and their job security than were the men. Possibly as a result, they were more likely to have thought of leaving church employment, and less likely to anticipate always working for the church. Women administrators were significantly more dissatisfied with the policies of the church, whether measured in the overall dissatisfaction or in the individual questions that composed it. They were also more likely to say that they would not be treated fairly in grievances.

Regrettably, similar analysis could not be done to compare the attitudes of black and white respondents. The overall variations in the employees' and administrators' estimations of the church's affirmative action efforts in this regard is more likely a simple artifact of their overall satisfaction or (especially) dissatisfaction with the church than a reflection of real situations. Still, with regard to the opportunities and remuneration enjoyed by women, in the eyes of the women respondents to the NACPA survey, at least, the church as employer has much to accomplish to achieve equity.

---

* Additional tables may be consulted at the NACPA National Office.

Part II

Reflections on the Sociological Analysis

— *6* —

Training and Development
by Mary Ellen McClanaghan, Ph.D.

HISTORY

Training and development on the job is not a new concept. Formalized training can trace its roots to the apprentice system as it is recorded in the Babylonian Code of Hammurabi, 1800 B.C.E. This document laid out rules for the transfer of skills from one generation to the next (Carnevale et al, 1990). Training systems can be traced through the ages with changes occurring along with economic and technological advancement. In our own country preparation for entrance into World War II brought with it the "challenge to develop skilled line workers and supervisory personnel who had the coaching and training skills essential for motivating the work force" (Carnevale, 1990:27). During this period of our history, training took on central importance. By the end of the war the position of training director was considered a new profession. In the three and a half decades since, the issues related to training have mainly involved methodology, evaluation methods and calculating the return on the investment. Currently managers and trainers are meeting a new challenge as substantial changes in the composition of the work force become increasingly evident.

PURPOSE OF TRAINING AND DEVELOPMENT

Employers' concern and interest in the education and training of their employees in profit-making organizations is utilitarian. The initials R.O.I. are the by-line for every personnel administrator in these companies. The training function is measured by this factor alone—Return On Investment. Very little of the massive amount of printed material dealing with training discusses the importance that the employees place on this aspect of their job. Even less of the literature deals with how the

training function affects their level of job satisfaction. It has been as-
serted, however, that "when learning experiences are based on actual
job needs, employees frequently work to increase their proficiency in
the expectation that they will trigger immediate rewards in terms of
achievement, status, and earnings (Carnevale, 1990:29).

The Catholic Church is not a "for profit" organization. The skills
and knowledge of their employees do not have a direct impact on the
bottom line. Therefore, the issue of training takes on a different meaning in this setting. NACPA's document, "Just Treatment for Those Who
Work for the Church" notes:

> Currently Church officials speak of a need for a consistent life
> ethic, i.e. for the full development of persons at every stage of
> life . . . This demands also that Church administrators recog-
> nize their responsibility to create and maintain a just work en-
> vironment that encourages and supports this full development
> of all persons serving the Church" (1986:2).

Implicit in the mission of the Catholic Church is the full development of all of its members. This emphasis has been renewed in church
documents since the Second Vatican Council. This development is for
the sake of human dignity of the individual worker. Even Alvin Toffler
(1983) makes the point that every dollar that is put into new machines
ought to be matched by several dollars of investment in human capital
"in training, education, relocation, social rehabilitation, in cultural adaptation" (cited in Nadler and Nadler, 1989:54). This respect for the
individuals is not without its pay offs usually resulting in more efficient
and happy workers. It is clear from the response to the attitudinal study
that people who have chosen to work for the church consider their own
personal development an important aspect of their labors. Training, development, and continuing education opportunities offer an important
avenue for encouraging and supporting the "full development of all persons serving the Church."

DEFINITIONS

Before beginning to discuss the results of the NACPA study conducted by Gallup, it is important to distinguish between the terms:
training, development and continuing education. Frequently the words
"training and development" are used as a phrase, like a full name.
There are some people who disdain the use of the word training in relationship to people. "People aren't trained, they're developed" said a
seminar participant quoted in *Training* magazine (July, 1988:22). In
their book *Developing Human Resources*, Leonard and Zeace Nadler
have devoted a chapter to each of the terms: Training, Development,
and Education. They define training as "learning, provided by

employers to employees, that is related to their present jobs" (1989:47). Training "is provided with the intent that the learning will be used almost immediately" (1989:63).

Education as it is defined by the Nadlers refers to learning that "is designed to prepare individuals for a job different than the one currently held" (1989:61). This type of learning is directly related to career development. It is provided to assist employees to move into higher level jobs when they become available. There is a risk for the employer in offering education benefits, in as much as employees may go elsewhere with their newly acquired knowledge and skills.

Development is defined as "learning experiences, provided by employers to employees that are not job related . . . development refers to general growth" (1989:74-75). This category covers activities that can range from study of a foreign language to stress reduction techniques. Managers who are concerned mainly with immediate return on investment are likely to find development classes/sessions disconcerting to say the least. However, managers who are concerned with the overall self-development of their employees recognize the value that is returned to the organization in terms of increased motivation and self-actualized workers. These opportunities offer individuals the chance to release hidden potentials that may, in the future, provide benefits to the organization. The cover of the July 1990 issue of *Personnel Journal* documents the "Wellness Payoff." Coors brewery claims that they have a 600% return on every dollar spent on wellness programs.

FINDINGS OF THE SURVEY

There were very few questions on the survey that dealt directly with the issue of training, development and continuing education. The most direct question was Number 12 which asked: How important are each of the following aspects of career development and training to you?

The opportunity to take a sabbatical leave

Being able to maintain close contact with people in my job or field who are not working for the church

The opportunity to go back to school or college for further training

To be able to get a similar job in another parish or diocese
Promotion opportunities.

The telephone interviews asked Catholic laity: How important do you think it is for people who work for the church to have the following benefits: (they were asked to respond to each of the above categories) Very Important, Important, Not Too Important, or Not Important at All? Each part of this question deserves its own attention.

SABBATICAL LEAVE

Although the ideal of a sabbatical year has its roots in the Hebrew scripture (Exodus 23:10-11; Det. 15:1-3; Lev. 25:2-8; Jer. 34:8-22 and Neh. 10:32) it is more likely the influence of academia on the church as an employer that prompts this question. Sabbatical leaves are most common today in higher education to provide opportunities for up-dating skills and/or writing and research. It would be assumed that a sabbatical for a church worker would be for educational purposes. Using the definition given by the Nadlers, it would appear that a sabbatical leave for a church worker may well result in increased promotion expectations. More than likely sabbaticals would be provided with a specific job in mind, such as a position in the Tribunal. Otherwise new knowledge gained could be used in new areas of employment. It is not surprising that the respondents to this question differed greatly depending on status and current position held. Administrators (especially those who work for religious congregations) placed the greatest value on the opportunity for sabbatical leaves; 74% of administrators considered this to be at least "Fairly Important." Religious felt the strongest about this, 83%. Priests were close behind, 82%, while only 52% of lay/deacons ranked sabbatical leaves "Very Important" or "Fairly Important."

Table 1
Sabbatical Leave Administrators

	Total	Priests	Religious	Lay/deacon
Very Important	38%	52%	40%	23%
Fairly Important	36%	30%	43%	29%

The total percent of employees in professional and support staff positions who ranked sabbaticals at least "Fairly Important" was 66%. Status again divided the respondents: priests, 88%, religious, 79% lay/deacons, 56%.

Table 2
Sabbatical Leave

	Total	Priests	Religious	Lay/deacon
Very Important	33%	63%	43%	23%
Fairly Important	33%	25%	36%	33%

Both administrators and employees with the most education tended to feel the strongest about the value of a sabbatical leave. It may well be that the concept of a sabbatical far exceeds the educational needs and expectations of employees who have greater responsibility to home and family. While only 2% of priests and religious found this opportunity to be "Not at All Important," 13% of lay/deacons saw it that way. Catholic laity surveyed by phone supported the ideal of the concept; 49% ranked this opportunity to be "Very Important" and 37% thought it was "Fairly Important." It would be interesting to know how many church workers are offered the opportunity for sabbatical leaves. A recent study (Joseph) indicated that 50% of sisters in new ministries had been provided with a sabbatical paid for by their congregation. Some dioceses offer this benefit to priests as reward for years of service or when they are being prepared for new ministries. Scheet's study (1989) found that younger priests (77%) are more likely to value sabbatical leaves than do older priests (46%).

BEING ABLE TO MAINTAIN CONTACT WITH PEOPLE IN SIMILAR JOB OR FIELD

This question appears to have referred to contacts with members of professional associations which offer the structure and source for keeping up-dated in the field. The question may not have provided an adequate test for that information in that only 34% of all employees and 39% of all administrators indicated that they thought it was "Very Important."

Religious administrators who work for congregations felt the strongest about this value, 46% responded "Very Important," while only 22% of all employees who work in parish offices saw it "Very Important" to maintain contact with their work cohorts. Employees who minister in fields that have active professional associations were more likely to value this type of contact; 45% of those who work in youth, health care or charities and 42% of those in education ranked this as "Very Important."

OPPORTUNITY TO GO BACK TO SCHOOL

A total of 43% of all employees rated this opportunity to be "Very Important." The highest percentage of respondents to cite going back to

Table 3
Opportunity to Go Back to School/Employees

	Total	Priests	Religious	Lay/deacon
Very Important	43%	29%	40%	47%
Fairly Important	37%	45%	40%	34%

school as "Very Important" were lay employees (single and married), 47%.

In the study 36% of the lay employees are not college graduates, while all of the priest employees have at least a college degree and all but 3% of the religious have attained at least this level of education. In most cases it may be assumed that the dioceses have provided the college education for the priests, and religious congregations have paid the price of the education for the religious. This lack of equity in educational experience also means that religious and priests are more highly educated for the same positions held by lay employees. Since more education is not likely to lead to a higher salary for priests, this may account for the fact that only 29% of priest employees rated this benefit "Very Important."

The religious appear to be interested in this benefit whether or not it brings a better pay check; 40% felt the opportunity for more schooling was "Very Important."

Age was also a significant factor in the response to this question. The correlation between the response "Very Important" and age is as follows: 64% of employees under 35; 46% of employees between 35-49; 32% of employees 50-64; 23% of employees over 65.

Table 4
Opportunity to Go Back to School\Employees\Age

	-35	35-49	50-64	65+
Very Important	64%	46%	32%	23%
Fairly Important	30%	37%	38%	33%

It is also interesting to note that only 37% of employees without a college degree rated this opportunity as "Very Important" in contrast to 52% of employees with a college degree. The number declines again with respondents with postgrad status. It may be that those without college degrees are also in the over 50 age brackets. Employees in the highest salary range (30K+) were the most likely to rate going back to school as "Very Important." When employees are looked at by field, 52% in youth and health and charities and 50% in education credited the opportunity to go back to school as "Very Important." Office personnel at the diocesan and parish level put substantially less importance on this advantage, 39% and 29% respectfully.

Although it would be an exaggeration to claim an overwhelming response to the importance of this benefit, it should be noted that few rated this as "Not Important at All." The greatest number who see no importance were diocesan employees, 6% and 5% of lay/deacons. It could be that older workers, near retirement in entry level positions fall into this category. From the trends that are cited by forecasters today these workers will not be replaced by like-minded workers.

A substantial difference is seen in the way administrators answered this question. Only 37% of all administrators thought the opportunity to go back to school was "Very Important." This represents 39% of both religious and lay administrators and 30% of priest administrators answered this way. Unlike employees, those without a college degree were most interested; 41% rated this benefit "Very Important."

Age again is a strong determinant; 70% of administrators under 35 cited this as "Very Important." This response decreases with advancing age. There is nearly a 30 point drop in the next age bracket.

Gender also has some bearing on response to this aspect of the question; 33% of females in contrast to 18% of males saw the opportunity to go back to school as "Very Important."

Catholic laity (75%) interviewed by phone regarded the opportunity to go back to school a "Very Important" benefit for workers in the church. Again the younger respondents felt the strongest; 82% of the 18-34 age bracket answered "Very Important." Less than 1% of all laity sampled saw "No Importance at All" for this benefit. These statistics support the growing trend of the population to place greater importance on college education (Johnson and Packer, 1990).

Table 5
Opportunity to Go Back to School\Administrators

	Total	Priests	Religious	Lay/deacon
Very Important	37%	30%	39%	39%
Fairly Important	38%	37%	42%	32%

It is interesting to compare how this question correlates with part five of Question 3. Part five of Question 3 asks respondents to rate their present benefit of reimbursement for educational expenses. Of all administrators 19% claimed they do not enjoy this benefit. Status appears to play a role in distribution of this benefit: 11% of priests, 17% of religious and 27% of lay/deacons do not receive education reimbursement.

Table 6
Opportunity to Go Back to School\Administrators\Age

	-35	35-49	50-64	65+
Very Important	70%	41%	32%	29%
Fairly Important	22%	38%	40%	38%

In the employees' responses, 34% of lay employees and 30% of all employees claimed they have no reimbursement at all for education.

For employees gender appears to be the significant variable; 21% of males did not have this benefit but 37% of females did not. The lowest record for reimbursement for educational expenses was for employees who work for congregations; 40% claimed they receive no reimbursement.

At the other end of the continuum are those who rated their reimbursement as "Excellent;" 21% of priest employees, 14% of religious employees and 8% of lay employees reported their reimbursement to be "Excellent." Administrators were not so enthusiastic. Only 2% rated this benefit as "Excellent."

Catholic laity responded to the question: "Tell me if you think people who work for the church probably receive Excellent, Good, Fair or Poor benefits for educational expenses." They responded in the following manner: Excellent- 9%, Good-22%, Fair-31%, Poor-18%, Don't know-19%. It has already been noted that 75% of these same respondents believe that it is a "Very Important" benefit for church workers to be able to go back to school.

Table 7
Reimbursement for Educational Expenses\Administrators

	Total	Priests	Religious	Lay/deacon
Excellent	3%	4%	2%	3%
Do Not Have	19%	11%	17%	27%

The issue raised by the responses to this question and its relationship to question 12 signals an important challenge to the church as an employer in the decades to come. Responses to both of these questions clearly indicate that the youngest of the respondents were the most eager for educational benefits. This is a sign of the times. Younger people are aware of the importance of education for their job prospects for the future. The recent publication of the study "Workforce 2000" cites the trend toward "higher education levels in each job category" (Johnson and Packer, 1990:98). The book *Megatrends 2000* calls baby-boomers "self-developers." The authors claim that this "archtype (self-developers) is even more prevalent among people in their early thirties and

Table 8
Reimbursement for Educational Expenses

Employees				
	Total	Priests	Religious	Lay/deacon
Excellent	11%	21%	14%	8%
Do Not Have	30%	7%	33%	34%

Gender		
	Females	Males
Do Not Have	37%	21%

twenties" (1990:222). The respondents to the NACPA survey are evidence of this fact. The issue of loyalty to the organization is also touched by this issue. "The new workforce will help your company achieve objectives if it can achieve its own personal goals as part of the bargain" (Naisbitt and Aburdene, 1990:223). Unless the church keeps pace with the growing demand for educated workers and provides the assistance needed to support educational expenses, it will be unlikely to attract bright young talent to fill open positions. The other consequence may be church workers who are among the least educated of the population.

ABILITY TO TRANSFER TO A SIMILAR POSITION IN ANOTHER DIOCESE OR PARISH

This issue appears to have little importance for most church workers. Only 25% of all administrators felt that this was "Very Important;" 33% felt it was "Fairly Important." Administrators in education, a field where there is traditionally more transferring from site to site, rated this more important than others; 32% of education administrators rated this "Very Important" in contrast to 22% of administrators in youth/health and charities. Only 20% of administrators in diocesan offices rated this as "Very Important." Religious were the most likely to look upon this type of an opportunity as career development potential; 32% consider this "Very Important" while only 16% of priests and 22% of lay/deacons answered this way. Once again age plays a significant role in answering this question; 57% of administrators under 35 considered this "Very Important," only 28% in the 35-49 age bracket and 21% in the 50-64 age bracket. The percent rises again to 29% for those over 65.

Some difference in the responses to this question may be found in status. Priests are usually ordained for a diocese, for them a move to a new diocese means more than mere relocation. Religious, on the other hand, usually have membership in various parts of the country and commonly move from place to place. Another explanation may be positions. Administration on the diocesan level is considered an executive position in the church. Older administrators who have been in the diocesan system for some time are likely to lose more than they would gain by transferring out of the diocese. These positions frequently provide vacation and pension benefits based on years of service to the diocese not the national church. Younger administrators, on the other hand, may not be vested and would gain wider recognition and bargaining power by moving.

Employees, like administrators, did not rate the ability to transfer to a similar position as important as other aspects of the question; 31% rated the opportunity to get a similar job in another parish or diocese as "Very Important." Again both age and life style were significant factors in rating this importance. Religious were the most likely to seek this advantage, 37%. Those employees under 35 years of age rated this more important (35%) than any other age bracket.

PROMOTION OPPORTUNITIES

The issue of promotion is greatly affected by two existing situations and two emerging situations. The existing situations are 1) the flatness of the organization and 2) the fact that most of the top positions are open only to the ordained. Priests hold 64% of the top diocesan jobs (Conscience, 1988) and close to 100% of all top parish positions.

Priests move to the top of their ladders basically on two tracks. These tracks are generally determined during seminary training. One track is determined on ability. The priests on this track are sent to elite graduate schools in preparation for chancery positions and with the possibility of hierarchy status in their future. All other priests are on track two which tops off at the level of pastor. This ladder is climbed on a seniority basis, despite the fact that 78% of the priests in the Peterson and Schoenherr study preferred promotion based on ability. In light of these existing facts it is not surprising that a mere 26% of administrators see promotion opportunities as "Very Important."

The two emerging situations, however, also affect the response to this question. 1) The growing shortage of priests (A 1984 study published by the National Conference of Catholic Bishops reports a 41% decline in diocesan seminarians). 2) The nature of the changing work force within the church especially the attitude of young workers, who are "self-developers."

The growing shortage of priests of course will necessitate the opening of the top level positions to the non-ordained. The changing

Table 9
Promotion\Age

Administrators				
	-35	35-49	50-64	65+
Very Important	57%	28%	21%	29%
Fairly Important	30%	35%	38%	27%

Employees				
	-35	35-49	50 - 64	65+
Very Important	55%	42%	30%	13%
Fairly Important	30%	33%	32%	28%

attitude of the new workers will demand a new look at educational and promotion policies. The study conducted for NACPA by Gallup gives evidence of this; 57% of administrators under 35 rated promotion opportunities as "Very Important" and 55% of employees in this age bracket concurred. Likewise this issue was most important to the lay/deacon workers.

Responses to importance of promotion from administrators are divided by status: Priests-17%, Religious-24% Lay/deacons-37% answered that promotion opportunities are "Very Important." The category "Fairly Important" may tell more of the story. When the numbers of these two categories are combined everyone seems more interested: Priests-47%, Religious-61% and Lay/deacons-75%.

Gender contributes to the difference when the two categories are combined; 69% of all female administrators rated promotion opportunities as at least "Fairly Important." Only 55% of all males (mostly priests) answered this way.

More employees, 38%, credited promotion as "Very Important." Status again is a significant factor: 46% of the lay workers, 26% of the religious and only 17% of priests answered "Very Important." Once again age makes the greatest contribution to the variance; 55% of all employees under the age of 35 rated promotion opportunities as "Very Important." The percentages decline as age advances. It is surprising to note that employees who earn the least, under 15K, have the smallest percent of respondents who consider promotion to be "Very Important." The Catholic laity who answered the same question regarding the importance of promotion opportunities for church workers take a much stronger position; 60% answered they thought promotion opportunities are "Very Important" and another 30% answered "Fairly Important."

CHALLENGES

There are two very clear points that emerge from reviewing the above detailed data. One point is that Catholic laity from the general population who were interviewed by phone want the workers in the church to have every advantage regarding education and career advancement. It can be assumed that the Catholic laity realize that these opportunities cost money. Money for this purpose ultimately comes from the same laity. The second point is that the youngest workers (those under 35) differ in their expectations from those of the older workers. They appear to mirror their age cohorts that are described as self developers, who are willing to work hard for an organization that offers them the opportunity to grow and develop. What the study does not reveal is just how much support is presently being given to these young workers. The one question that does present a picture of what is actually happening regarding educational reimbursement does not appear promising. It is not surprising that 39% of young administrators and 28% of young employees have given a "Great deal" of thought to leaving church employment in the last 12 months. Clearly, the greatest challenge that the church as employer will meet in the coming decade is how to attract and keep workers. Studies show that money is not the greatest motivator for these new workers. Career development is more important to today's young workers than money or organizational loyalty (Sutcliffe and Schuster, 1985).

Table 10
Promotion\Administrators

	Total	Priests	Religious	Lay/deacon
Very Important	26%	17%	24%	37%
Fairly Important	35%	30%	37%	38%

"One of the most consistent findings from recent studies of 'excellent companies' in both the private and public sector, has been that these organizations are distinctive" (Posner and Schmidt, 1988:23-24). The Catholic Church certainly has the potential to be a distinctive employer. Distinctive organizations have a clarity of mission and that mission is understood by employees at every level of the organization. "One unambiguous, consistent message and practice in excellent organizations is that people matter" (Posner and Schmidt, 1988:25). The business world is well aware of the importance of investing in their employees. Motorola requires that 1.5 percent of payroll is spent on training and education of their employees. "American business is spending $210 billion for on-the job training and education, a system about the same size as the nation's public elementary, secondary, and higher education institutions combined" (Naisbitt and Aburdene, 1990:228-229). This should be viewed in light of 30% of respondents to the NACPA study claiming to receive no reimbursement for educational expenses.

As the traditional church minister changes, it becomes more and more imperative to have a well organized system for on-going training of both new and experienced church workers. It can no longer be assumed that the seminary and the sister formation program have prepared workers for the vineyard. A 1984 study published by the National Conference of Catholic Bishops reported a 41% decline in diocesan seminarians and an 86% decline in new entrants to women's religious congregations (Costello, 1987). The average worker in the church in the coming decade is sure to be a lay person and many of them will be from minority groups. The NACPA study conducted by Gallup indicates that respondents from all categories surveyed give the church poor grades for their ability to hire and or promote minorities, and there is some evidence that promotion of women also is in need of adjustment.

These facts in themselves are evidence of the need for greater education and training within the church community. It has been documented that educational reimbursement for priests (still the chief decision makers) is better than for any other group of church worker. Some other studies have indicated that the money available to priests for education may not be spent. Fogarty (1988) reported that only 13% of priests in the Joliet diocese "Very frequently" availed themselves of continuing education opportunities.

The NACPA study signals that education is a key element in insuring competent workers for the church of tomorrow. Catholic laity put a high regard on having educated leaders and presumably will be willing to pay for the cost of competence. The youngest workers presently working in the church recognize the importance of continuing education and are unlikely to be satisfied with less. NACPA is taking the initiative to insure that its membership and their employees are well equipped to meet the growing demands of the changing work environment. The annual convocation is a showcase of training and education for personnel administrators which hopefully influences the practices of participants back home. NACPA offers a wide variety of workshops and consultation services to assist members in providing services to church workers. On-going publications keep members current on topics of importance. Many other associations offer expert training services on local levels. It remains in the hands of decision makers, however, to assure that the training, development and continuing education needs of their employees are annually reassessed. As long as the majority of decision-makers, therefore hiring agents, are priests, the first challenge is to educate these decision makers to meet the new challenges. Only 30% of all of the priest administrators thought that the opportunity to go back to school was "Very Important."

Taylor (1985) in his discussion of power in the work place makes the point that training and development for supervisory and management positions ought to be prepared for in advance of position openings. "Outstanding line workers should be exposed to supervisory development before they are placed in the hot spot . . . Outstanding supervisors should be receiving management development . . ." He further notes that failure to invest in training and development of future supervisors and managers is "setting up power failures as a matter of policy" (p. 49).

CONCLUSION

Failure on the part of the Catholic Church to recruit and promote minorities and women promises to result in an organization that will not be able to hire or retain competent loyal workers in the future. Successful organizations of the future will respond "creatively to filling the knowledge gap . . . and hire broadly educated people and upgrade the cultural and technical literacy of its work force . . ." (Coates, Jarratt and Mahaffie, 1990:295).

— 7 —

Recruitment, Retention, Job Descriptions, Performance Appraisals
by Lucien Roy, STL

The main focus of the last century's church documents on issues of social justice and work-related themes has concentrated primarily on issues of compensation, the dignity of the human person, conditions within the workplace and the rights of workers to associate.

The efforts of NACPA have been in a consistent line with this tradition of social teaching. In particular, NACPA has tried to promote the development and observance of consistent policies and practices with respect to those individuals who are employed by the church. As articulated in *Just Treatment for Those Who Work for the Church*, NACPA has consistently dedicated itself to the promotion of a comprehensive personnel system. By this is meant: "A comprehensive approach to church personnel administration includes both the variety of people serving the church (lay people, sisters, brothers, deacons and priests) and the range of personnel functions (recruitment, selection, training, formation, policy development, salary administration, benefits, due process, termination and retirement)." (*Just Treatment*, 1986:1)

In pursuing this development of a comprehensive approach, NACPA has stressed that "justice urges us to recognize that the treatment of one category of persons has direct implications for the treatment of others." (*Just Treatment*, 1986:1)

Other articles in this series have concentrated on other issues which were examined by the survey. In this article three areas were examined from the attitudinal survey.

Two of these areas are very specific. One of them pertains to the existence of clear job descriptions for individual positions and duties. The second of those is related to the first and concentrates on the practice of annual performance appraisals.

The third area is indeed a much broader and complex pattern of many issues. Specifically, that area is the one of recruitment and retention of employees within the church system. While there are some direct questions contained in the survey which focus on this topic, there is a web of converging factors which needs to be examined if one is to gain insights into the present performance and future promise of recruitment and retention within the church.

For the sake of clarity, it seems easiest to deal with the two discreet issues first and then to move on to the pattern of factors related to recruitment and retention.

CLEAR JOB DESCRIPTIONS

As institutions have become more and more bureaucratized, there has been greater insistence upon providing clear descriptions of roles and responsibilities for individual positions. One aim of this insistence has been to provide for agreed upon criteria of accountability in order to assure quality performance and production. A concomitant result of clear job descriptions is a measure of protection for the employee against the potential of arbitrary evaluation.

Despite the benefits of having clear job descriptions both for the institution and for the individual there is an ongoing argument about whether the benefits mentioned above outweigh the need for flexibility and shared responsibility. NACPA's position is that accurate and current job descriptions containing clear lines of accountability need to be available." (*Just Treatment*, 1986:9)

Considerable efforts have been made to establish clear job descriptions for positions within the church. One example of this is the collection of ministry profiles in *Coordinating Parish Ministries* published by the Archdiocese of Chicago.

Among the core assumptions established as the basis for a comprehensive approach to compensation for church workers, NACPA holds: "Each church institution has developed an operative plan including a mission statement. It knows what specific need it is fulfilling by individual positions within the institution." (*Pathfinder*, 1989:22)

Another reason for the importance of establishing job or position descriptions is in reference to issues of internal equity among positions within a church institution. The NACPA document states that each position within the institution is valued as contributing to the well-being of the institution. Therefore, a job or position description is to be developed for all positions and used as the basis of setting the criteria for hiring and of establishing the range for the appropriate wage. (*Pathfinder*, 1989:23)

FINDINGS OF THE SURVEY

One of the items in the survey inquired about the provision of such clear job descriptions. In exploring this issue, there were different vantage points for the responses from either administrators or employees. The focus of the question was different for administrators (those workers with supervisory responsibilities) than it was for employees (professional and support staff).

The administrators were asked to state whether or not they agreed with the statement, "We have a clear description of job duties and functions for most positions." The employees, on the other hand, were asked whether or not they agreed with the personal statement, "I have a clear description of my job duties and functions."

There was general agreement between the administrators and the employees about the provision of clear job descriptions. (See Table 1)

TABLE 1

	Administrators describe all positions	Employees describe own position
5 - Agree completely	25%	39%
4	43%	34%
3	19%	14%
2	8%	7%
1 - Disagree completely	2%	4%
No answer	2%	2%

When the responses of administrators and employees were compared with regard to the place or field of employment, several interesting observations came to light. Among those working for dioceses, approximately 70% of both administrators and employees agreed that there were clear job descriptions. There was comparable agreement between employees and administrators who work in diocesan offices, in education and in health/youth ministry/charities. However, for those working in parish settings, there was a significant difference between the response of the administrators and of the employees. The employees were much less likely (12%) to say that they had clear job descriptions than the parish administrators were to say that they provided them.

When the place of employment was a religious congregation, there was again a significant difference between the responses from the administrators and the employees. In this setting, however, the employees were more likely to say that they had job descriptions than the administrators were to say that they provided them. (See Table 2)

TABLE 2
% With Job Descriptions

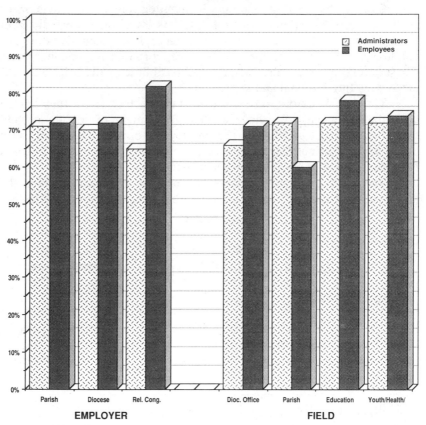

ADMINISTRATORS

When the administrators were examined from the vantage point of site of employment and field of ministry, several interesting patterns emerged.

First of all, when administrators who responded in agreement to the statement about providing clear descriptions of job duties and functions for most positions were viewed with regard to parish, diocese or congregation, the following results were evident:

Degree of agreement

	Parish	Diocese	Congregation
5 - agree completely	21%	30%	18%
4 -	50%	39%	46%

While the composite scores in these two highest degrees of agreement were fairly equal, the number of administrators in the diocesan arena who agreed most strongly was significantly larger than for those administrators working in either parish or congregational settings.

The next vantage point from which the responding administrators were viewed was that of the field of ministry. The percentages of agreement in these instances were as follows:

Degree of agreement

	Diocesan office	Parish office	Education	Youth/Health/ Charities
5 - agree completely	28%	21%	27%	37%
4 -	38%	51%	45%	46%

When the mean scores were compared according to field, it was evident that there was a greater possibility of providing clear job descriptions in the field of youth/health/charities, secondly in education, next, somewhat surprisingly, parish offices, and finally, diocesan offices. Those mean scores respectively were youth/health/charities (4.09), education (3.95), parish office (3.83), diocesan office (3.80).

Employees

When the responses of the employees alone were examined according to status, the percentages of those who were in agreement with the statement of having a clear job description were as follows: lay employees 74%, priests 66%, religious 75%. The priests were considerably less likely to be provided with clear job descriptions.

Additional Findings Regarding Clarity Of Job Description

1. Those employees with clear job descriptions were somewhat less likely to be thinking of changing their jobs even though most (75%) felt they could easily find one.

2. Employees with clear job descriptions were also more likely to say that they were part of a vibrant church community.

3. There was also a positive co-relation between an employee having a clear job description and believing that his or her long-term future is secure.

4. This positive co-relation also held between one's clear job description and sense of security even if leadership or one's own supervisor were to change.

Reflections

Two significant observations from the responses pertaining to job descriptions are as follows:

1. A large discrepancy exists between the responses of parish administrators (pastors) and parish employees on whether the employees receive job descriptions.

2. Priests, as a group, were far less likely to receive a clear description of the role and functions of their jobs.

The significance of having a clear job description, in reference to issues of recruitment and retention, will be explored later in this article. The implications of priests being far less likely to have clear job descriptions needs to be explored further in the context of the desirability of a genuinely comprehensive personnel system. The consequences with regard to accountability and to vulnerability on the part of the employee without a clear job description deserve further study.

ANNUAL PERFORMANCE APPRAISAL

NACPA's policy with regard to performance evaluation is quite clear. "Performance evaluation procedures are essential to a just working environment as well as to the full development of persons. Fair and honest performance evaluation is to occur at regular, predetermined intervals for all church personnel." (*Just Treatment*, 1986:9)

Indeed it is the position of NACPA that evaluation is an integral component of compensation. "An evaluation process for all church workers is part of the compensation system." (*Pathfinder*, 1989:22)

The position paper went on to stipulate the components of such an evaluation and the manner in which it should be conducted. The question in the survey pertaining to performance evaluation made no stipulations about the nature or extent of the evaluations. Therefore, the responses may reflect a varied understanding of the type of "evaluation" to which the respondents were referring.

FINDINGS OF THE SURVEY

Here again, the questions were worded differently for administrators and employees. The administrators were asked to state whether or not they gave job performance evaluations at least once a year. The employees, on the other hand, were asked to state whether or not they themselves received a job performance evaluation at least once a year.

Of the total number or responding administrators, 54% agreed that they provided for annual performance evaluation. Of the employees, 48% agreed that they received annual evaluations. It is when the responses are studied with regard to the place and field of employment that significant findings emerge. (See Table 3)

TABLE 3
% with Performance Appraisals

When the place of employment or the field of ministry was the parish, there was a wide discrepancy between the responses of the administrators and those of the employees. In each instance, the administrators were far more likely to claim that they provided performance evaluations, while the employees stated that they did not receive them.

Just the obverse is true when the setting was that of the religious congregation. In that instance, far more employees indicated that they received performance evaluations than administrators indicated that they provided them.

The discrepancies in both parish and religious congregation settings may reflect different understandings of what is entailed in "performance evaluation." Whatever the source of the discrepancy, the diverging views between administrators and employees require further exploration and clarification.

When the responses of the employees alone were further compared according to status, the following patterns emerged. The percentages of employees who agreed with receiving annual performance evaluations were: lay 55%, priests 19%, religious 47%. The employees from each of these three groupings who responded categorically that they did not receive an annual evaluation were: lay 22%, priests 48%, religious 22%.

Administrators

When the responding administrators were broken down into subcategories according to the arena in which they work, the top levels of agreement were as follows:

Degree of agreement

	Parish	Diocese	Congregation
5 - agree completely	22%	36%	25%
4 -	29%	19%	26%

When reviewing the mean scores according to arena of employment, there was a strong parallel position for diocese (3.50) and congregation (3.49) and a fairly large falling off in the mean response from the setting of the parish (3.13)

Again, when studying the administrators responses according to the field of ministry in which they worked, there was a clear pattern of the consistent presence of performance evaluations. In descending order, the mean responses by field were as follows: Youth/Health/Charities (3.95); Education (3.64); Diocesan Office (3.42); Parish Office (3.00).

Here again, there was a rather marked difference between certain specific fields, such as youth/health/charities and the parish office, with regard to performance evaluations. In general, both in the area of performance evaluations and job descriptions, the field of parish ministries seems to need increased professionalization.

Additional Findings Regarding Occurrence Of Performance Evaluation

1. There was a strong relationship between performance evaluation and job clarity for employees. Those who disagreed with one of these two statements were far more likely to disagree with the other as well and those who agreed with one were more likely to agree with the other.

2. Significant patterns also appeared in the relationship between performance evaluations and field of ministry with employees in parish

offices being significantly less likely to agree that they received these evaluations and charities and youth ministries more likely to receive them.

3. When parish employees were compared to all other respondents, lay employees were more likely to say that they did not receive performance evaluations.

Challenges

The most significant challenge to church personnel administrators with respect to performance appraisals is to continue to work in the direction of a genuinely comprehensive approach. There are very clear discrepancies in the patterns of the occurrence of performance appraisals. One of those was with respect to the place of employment in which the parish setting fell considerably below that of other ministerial settings. The second major discrepancy and indeed the most dramatically different percentage of responses was between priests, religious and lay workers in which the priests were far less likely to receive performance evaluations. Inequity in the implementation of appraisal policies is in direct contrast to an espoused preference for a comprehensive approach to personnel issues.

RECRUITMENT

The future of any institution is contingent upon its ability to recruit and retain quality employees. The effectiveness of the church as an employer in this area of recruitment needs to be examined from two vantage points. The first of these is that of the administrators who themselves have the responsibility of attracting new employees into the institution. The second grouping, clearly, are those potential employees who themselves are the object of the recruiting efforts.

FINDINGS OF THE SURVEY

The survey focused directly on this issue of recruitment only from the vantage point of the supervisors or administrators. The administrators were asked to indicate the degree to which they agreed or disagreed with this statement: "We are able to hire and retain qualified employees."

The responses by the administrators to this question were basically positive. As a whole, their responses were as follows:

Degree of Agreement

5 (Agree completely)	21%
4	38%
3	25%
2	10%
1 (Disagree completely)	3%

The mean response of the administrators on this scale of 1 to 5 was 3.66.

When the mean response of the administrators was examined with regard to certain subgroupings, the following picture emerged. The male respondents (3.72) were more positive than the female administrators (3.59). The older the administrator, the more likely he or she was to be in agreement with the statement. The higher the level of education attained by the administrator, the more likely he or she was to be in agreement with the statement. There was no real difference in response as determined by the region of the country. The most significant variation depended on the status of the administrator. There was a definite difference of opinion concerning the ability to hire and retain qualified employees between the priests (3.96), the vowed religious (3.70) and the lay administrators (3.32).

There was no significant difference between the responses of administrators working for parishes, dioceses or religious congregations.

There was a relationship between the administrators' perceived ability to hire and retain qualified employees and whether they themselves were thinking of changing jobs. Those administrators who perceived themselves as unable to hire or retain good employees were more likely to be thinking of changing jobs themselves.

The more dissatisfied the administrator felt, either with his or her own salary or with the salaries that "church workers" in general received, the more likely he or she was to feel hindered in this regard.

Perceived ability to hire and retain qualified employees was similarly related to the administrators' total ranking of the benefits received by employees.

Administrators who thought employees felt insecure were also more likely to complain that they could not hire or retain qualified workers.

No corresponding question pertaining to recruitment in general was asked of the employees who participated in the survey. The employees as well as the administrators were asked to evaluate the church's efforts in recruiting various minorities. This topic has been developed in greater detail in the chapter on affirmative action.

The telephone survey of the laity at large began by inquiring whether or not the respondents would be happy if a close relative of theirs chose to work for the church. On the scale of 1 to 4, the mean response was 3.50 indicating a very high level of agreement. Thus there is a generally supportive atmosphere among Catholics which would encourage a positive response on the part of future potential employees to recruitment efforts on the part of the church as employer.

CHALLENGES

One of the motivating factors at work in attracting individuals to employment in the church is a sense of personal vocation. The survey did not focus directly on that dimension of the process of recruitment. This very significant aspect of working for the church needs further study particularly as it relates to lay employees.

There has been considerable research literature focusing on recruitment to the life-style of a priest or vowed religious. Very little research has focused on the recruitment of individuals from within either of those life-styles to a particular job or position within the church. As the church in its role of employer looks to the future, it will need to refine its understanding of its role as that of recruiting people for particular areas of responsibility.

RETENTION

Effective recruitment without successful retention threatens the future of any institution. With regard to retention, as well as to recruitment, two vantage points need to be considered. The first of these is the attitude and expectations of the employees. The second is the effort on the part of the institution to create a setting and to provide incentives that result in a positive decision on the part of the employee to remain with the institution.

An employee's decision to remain in his/her position is indeed a complex blend of many factors. Refer to the other articles in this series for a composite picture of the tangible dimensions such as compensation and benefits and the more intangible factors such as opportunities for training and the climate of affirmative action.

FINDINGS OF THE SURVEY

In the survey there was one specific question relating to retention that was asked both of administrators and employees. Each of the groups was asked about expectations pertaining to their own future.

They were asked to reply whether they regarded the statement "I expect to work always for the church" as true or not.

The responses were as follows:

TABLE 4
Expectation of Always Working for the Church

Degree of Truth	Administrators	Employees
4 - very true	48%	32%
3 - fairly true	30%	37%
2 - not very true	14%	19%
1 - not at all true	6%	9%
no answer	2%	2%

When the administrators and employees were broken down into subgroupings according to status, there was a dramatic difference in their responses. (See Table 5)

In terms of the shifting percentages of priests, religious and lay workers working in the church, considerable attention will need to be paid to the work expectations of the lay workers. It can no longer be taken for granted that once an individual is working for the church he or she will always remain in that position.

TABLE 5
Expectation of Always Working for the Church

Degree of Truth	Administrators			Employees		
	Priests	Religious	Lay	Priests	Religious	Lay
4 - very true	78%	47%	22%	72%	54%	16%
3 - fairly true	16%	35%	35%	17%	28%	45%
2 - not very true	2%	12%	27%	5%	13%	24%
1 - not at all true	1%	4%	13%	—	3%	13%
no answer	2%	2%	2%	5%	2%	1%

There might have been a negative assumption that lay people would remain working for the church because they would not be able to find, with ease, a comparable position working for another employer. The responses to the question "How easy would it be for you to find a position outside of the Church with comparable or better pay than you are receiving now?" were as follows:

Table 6
Ease of Finding New Position

	Administrators	Employees
4 - very easy	32%	26%
3 - fairly easy	44%	44%
2 - fairly difficult	10%	11%
1 - very difficult	3%	2%
not sure	10%	14%
no answer		2%

Within the subgroupings by status, there was little significant difference in the responses depending on whether one was a priest, religious or lay person.

These attitudes among administrators and employees within the church were also mirrored in the attitudes of the laity at large. Among the laity polled through the telephone survey, 22% indicated that they believed it would be very easy for people working for the church to find a job outside the church with the same or better pay and 52% indicated that it would be at least fairly easy. So over all, 77% of the laity at large were in agreement with that statement. Employees who work for the church both think of themselves and are regarded by others as having ease of access to employment in other circumstances.

Another dimension of crucial importance to those examining the potential for retaining quality employees within the church is whether or not those same employees are themselves thinking of leaving church employ.

This aspect also was examined in questions posed both to administrators and to employees. Each of them was asked, "In the past twelve months, how much thought if any have you given to leaving church employment and finding employment elsewhere?"

Among the lay workers, both for administrators and employes, a considerable number of individuals especially under the age of 50 have given at least some and in many cases a great deal of thought to finding

TABLE 7
Thought Given to Leaving Church Employment
(Administrators)

Amount of thought	Administrators	Priests	Religious	Lay	Under 35	35-49	50-64	65+
A great deal	13%	4%	10%	28%	39%	18%	8%	6%
Some	20%	11%	22%	25%	9%	27%	15%	9%
Very little	21%	15%	24%	21%	26%	19%	23%	15%
None at all	41%	64%	42%	18%	22%	35%	47%	50%
I am too old to change now	3%	2%	2%	6%				21%
No answer	2%	4%	1%	3%				

TABLE 8
Thought Given to Leaving Church Employment
(Employees)

Amount of thought	Administrators	Priests	Religious	Lay	Under 35	35-49	50-64	65+
A great deal	16%	5%	8%	21%	28%	20%	8%	0%
Some	28%	14%	21%	34%	37%	30%	26%	8%
Very little	20%	21%	18%	20%	24%	22%	17%	8%
None at all	27%	55%	44%	16%	11%	25%	32%	46%
I am too old to change now	5%	3%	6%	6%			12%	28%
No answer	3%	1%	2%	4%			4%	10%

employment elsewhere. Particular attention will need to be paid to determining and providing those tangible and intangible factors which will persuade the employees to continue working for the church.

Clearly one dimension of those persuasive factors pertain to the security that persons feel as they contemplate their long-term future. A series of questions pertaining to security were posed both to administrators and employees. A review of the responses by status indicates that the lay workers were consistently and in many cases substantially less secure than priests or vowed religious when contemplating either their long-term future, the possibility of a change in church leadership, a change in their immediate supervisor. Lay employees were also much less secure as they contemplated the possibility of being incapacitated or as they faced the need to provide for their own retirement.

Lay workers and religious shared the thought that there may come a day when they will no longer be able to afford to continue working for the church. On a scale of 1 (not at all secure) to 4 (very secure), the mean responses on this issue were: lay = 2.85; priests = 1.46; religious = 2.36.

Intangible Factors

The employees were asked a question worded as follows: "I participate in decisions about my job and workplace conditions." There was no parallel question asked of the administrators. Because numerous studies have indicated that the degree of participation in decision making is a critical factor in determining one's satisfaction with one's work setting, it is important to consider these responses when examining retention of employees. On the scale of 1 (disagree completely) to 5 (agree completely), the mean response for all of the employees was 3.88. When that grouping was broken down by status, the mean scores reflected were: lay employees (3.88); priests (3.76); religious (3.93). When examined from the vantage point of the site of employment, the highest level of agreement with the statement on participation was reflected by those who work for a religious congregation (4.05), followed by the parish setting (3.99) and finally by those in a diocesan setting (3.76).

Other intangible factors with regard to retention of employees include a sense of responsibility, a sense of recognition and good relationships with one's co-workers.

When the degree of satisfaction with the responsibility which one has been given was examined according to status, the mean responses on a 4 point scale in an ascending order were: lay workers (3.53), religious (3.61) and priests (3.71).

When that same scale was used to measure satisfaction with the recognition one receives for one's work, that break down by status was as follows: priests (2.97), lay employees (3.04) and religious (3.27).

When the degree of satisfaction inquired after was that of one's relations with one's co-workers, the breakout according to status was: lay employees (3.48), priests (3.49) and religious (3.58).

In general then, the characteristics of responsibility, recognition and relationships with one's co-workers were not substantially different depending upon one's marital status. With regard to these characteristics of the work culture within the church then, there has been some considerable success in reaching a genuinely comprehensive approach to personnel practices.

Other Observations

Employees who rated their salaries as good or excellent with respect to their own or their family needs were more likely to anticipate always working for the church.

As Table 9 shows, a summed rating of total benefits together with salary comparability was consistently related to employees' anticipation of always working for the church.

For both employees and administrators, there was a positive co-relation between expected continuing employment in the church and the length of time they had already worked for the church as well as their own enthusiasm about the church.

The lay respondents, both administrators and employees, who felt the clergy were reluctant to share their duties were much less likely to expect always to work for the church.

Challenges

The responsibility for retaining employees rests firmly with the employing institution. As church employers review the factors creating a favorable climate for retention, they will need to pay particular attention to the issues of salary and benefits discussed at length in this series in the article on Compensation. They will need also to give very serious consideration to "career development" and its importance to church

TABLE 9
% Expecting Always to Work for the Church (Employees)

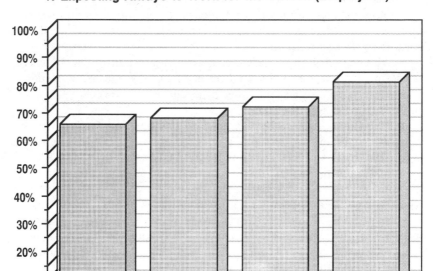

RATING OF BENEFITS

workers. This latter issue is treated in this series in the article on Training and Development. Of particular importance, given the large percentage of church workers who are female, will be the response on the part of the church to women's issues. For the significance of the survey responses on this topic, see the companion article on Affirmative Action.

A review of the survey results gives some clear indications of areas calling for concrete responses: increase in salary and benefit packages; attention to employment security concerns; expanded opportunities for women; increased support for training and development.

Beyond this, the church as employer would do well to study further the implications of understanding church work in particular on the part of lay persons in the context of vocation. This dimension along with other intangibles, such as increased participation in decision-making processes, are key ingredients for retention as well as the more tangible aspects of salary and benefits.

CONCLUSION

The dramatic shifts which the church as employer has undergone in the past twenty-five years are monumental. The diminishment of the traditional pool of clergy and vowed religious and the off-setting increase in the numbers of lay persons now employed by the church have necessitated a complete renewal in the understanding of church personnel practices. This restructuring and indeed this attitudinal conversion has taken place in the midst of decreasing financial resources and increasing expectations on the part of a growing Catholic population.

Given all of these complexities, the church has made great strides in the direction of developing a comprehensive personnel system. There is clear evidence of attempts both to introduce professionalization and to provide for equitable treatment of all of its employees.

Nonetheless, there is considerable work which remains. Despite their importance, job descriptions are not yet uniformly in place. Performance appraisals are even less prevalent, and there is considerable disparity with regard to who receives them. The responsibility of attracting and retaining quality employees necessitates not only a new awareness on the part of church as employer but demands deliberate increased attentiveness to both tangible and intangible factors that make the church a worthwhile arena that is both attractive to and supportive of priests, religious and lay workers alike.

— 8 —

Employment Grievances

by

William P. Daly, MS

and

Ann Marie Winters, JCL

Like other human organizations, church workplaces occasionally experience breakdowns in communication, conflicts between employees, and offensive supervisory practices. Effective organizations encourage resolution of such problems lest they cause negative undercurrents in the workplace.

Church workplaces have typically provided employees with one of the following avenues of complaint resolution:

Due Process Systems: These have been established in many church organizations to resolve complaints against administrators. They focus on employment issues as well as other types of complaints (e.g., liturgical, pastoral). They include conciliation and arbitration by third parties who have no direct involvement in the conflict. Elaborate and complex procedures guide their use.

Internal Grievance Procedures: These have been set up in many church organizations to address employee complaints about working conditions and other aspects of employment. They typically involve a series of meetings between employees and supervisors and may include review, investigation, or mediation by specially assigned employees or committees.

Internal Grievance Procedures Ending in Due Process: These combine an internal process at the early stages of resolution with the due process system in the later, more formal stages.

Ad hoc Processing of Complaints: Some organizations have no formal procedures for complaint resolution. These rely on informal interaction between employees and administrators for the resolution of employee grievances.

In recent times, church policy has devoted careful attention and priority to justice issues within the institutional segment of church. As early as the 1960's, attention was being focused on increasing fairness and justice within the church. Protection of rights was seen as the vanguard of justice concerns, and the 1967 Synod of Bishops adopted a principle espousing the more effective protection of rights. The revision of the Code of Canon Law begun during this same era crafted a legal framework which bolsters the greater protection of rights in the church.

In the United States, members of the Canon Law Society of America (CLSA) responded to the United States Bishops' request to find a means of safeguarding and promoting the rights of Catholics. The proposed CLSA report "On Due Process" was adopted by U.S. Bishops in 1969. There has been a wide variety of experience in the U.S. with "due process." Three kinds of experiences have emerged: diocesan "due process"; "due process" through the diocesan education office; and "due process" in religious institutes. Within four years of its first approval by the National Conference of Catholic Bishops (NCCB) over 100 dioceses were reported to have adopted the "Due Process" plan (Kennedy, 135). The components of substantive and procedural due process were outlined as conciliation and arbitration. A 1985 report on a task force survey by the CLSA found that over 57 percent of the dioceses in the United States have had some experience with diocesan "due process," either in developing materials or in actually processing a case (Provost, 1985, 6). Following is a brief summary of the initial findings from the 1985 report of the three kinds of experiences of due process. This reflects the structures adopted between the 1970's and the early 1980's.

CURRENT CHURCH POLICY AND PRACTICE ON DISPUTE RESOLUTION

With the promulgation of the revised Code of Canon Law in 1983, there has been renewed interest in developing the structures which increase just treatment within the church. Besides the Code's orientation toward the dignity and equality of persons in the church, there is an extensive but not exhaustive list of the rights vindicated. Bishops are authorized to establish offices for mediation of conflicts (Canon 1933).

Canonists have identified and explored with interest the codal structures pertaining to protection and vindication of rights. The judicial forum which has been largely occupied with matrimonial concerns has been exploring the adjudication of rights issues (i.e., Court in Equity of the Archdiocese of Baltimore). A model ecclesiastical court in equity is functioning as part of the tribunal in the Archdiocese of Baltimore. It exists for the purpose of juridically resolving controversies, and it is staffed by masters in equity—retired civil judges and attorneys. A case is begun with a hearing, followed by "findings of fact." After hearing from all the parties, the master in equity submits written recommendations to the chief judge of the court who signs an "order" which is binding on all parties involved in the controversy.

Administrative recourse has been explained and made accessible to church members by a series of steps to be followed in registering complaints (cf. canons 1732-1752). The Diocese of La Crosse has simplified norms for administrative recourse. Administrative recourse differs from the judicial process as an alternate means for resolving conflicts in the church. It is particularly recommended for disputes between those who exercise pastoral authority and those who have felt injured by a pastoral decision or action. At the first step, the aggrieved party attempts the direct resolution of the difficulty with the authority in question. The canonical process of administrative recourse consists in a successive appeal, as necessary, to the various levels of pastoral authority in the church. Respecting subsidiarity, the appeal is made first to the most local pastoral authority who is best able to know the circumstances and persons and to suggest a way of reconciliation.

Various dioceses, such as Milwaukee and Minneapolis-St. Paul, have fine-tuned the conciliation and arbitration procedures which have provided alternate means of dispute resolution. In ordinary practice *conciliation* is thought to imply an unequal power relationship between the parties. The conciliator usually meets with the parties separately to explore the nature of the dispute and possible solutions. Then, meeting jointly, the conciliator guides the parties toward a peaceful settlement. If counsel is sought by one or both parties, counsel may be admitted during the course of proceedings in so far as they further the establishment of agreement and accord. If agreement is reached, it is recorded in a summary by the conciliator.

Arbitration is a more formal process and adds the distinct element of the parties accepting the decision of the arbitrator as final and binding. Evidence and arguments are presented by both parties during hearings; positions of each party are made known. Parties may be represented by counsel. The arbitrator is free to call in experts during the hearing. *Fact finding* may be used to draw out factual information from witnesses, thereby clarifying facts and evidence already brought to light. A *board of review*, whose members are trained in civil or canon law, is concerned only with examining procedural errors or inequities in the arbitration process. The board is empowered to sustain, reverse or modify a decision, or to order a rehearing before the same or different arbitrators.

Chancery administrators and tribunal judges have been concerned to effect greater justice within the executive (administrative) and judicial departments of diocesan government. Personnel directors in human resource departments have been developing structures for handling employee grievances. The result is a panoply of methods, models and procedures which are often confusing and not yet integrated for the easy access of church employees or church members.

The established policy of the church stresses the importance of addressing and resolving conflicts between church administrators and those affected by their decisions or actions. In its efforts to provide resources to church administrators, NACPA has consistently supported and facilitated this church personnel policy. In *Just Treatment for Those Who Work for the Church* (NACPA, 1986), NACPA identified grievance procedures as one of the key ingredients of a fair and effective workplace. Church organizations have been encouraged and assisted in developing written grievance procedures and other personnel policies in a number of NACPA publications.

While many positive impressions emerged from the survey, it also uncovered a troubling picture of employee perceptions about grievance handling in church organizations. The employees in the survey responded about their own expectations of treatment as workers. The administrators responded to questions about how fairly they felt employees would be treated. Only 40% of employees and 42% of administrators felt that employees would be treated justly in a legitimate grievance.

Further analysis of the survey data brings some necessary clarification but does not alter the picture. The statement to which employees responded read, "If I have a legitimate grievance about working conditions I am confident the church will treat me justly." Of those surveyed 10% disagreed completely with the statement; 20% disagreed to a lesser degree; 14% agreed completely; 26% disagreed to a lesser degree; 28% took a neutral position between disagreeing and agreeing; and 2% gave no answer. Thus only 40% answered the question with some level of agreement, while 30% answered the question with some level of disagreement and 30% were either neutral or gave no answer. While active belief in just treatment in the church was low, active belief that the church is unjust was lower. The large number of people who did not comment either way was a significant factor in keeping the overall positive evaluation of church just treatment low. The response patterns among administrators was similar, with 42% answering with some level of agreement, 25% answering with some level of disagreement and 33% remaining neutral.

The data can be further analyzed to see if certain groups of employees or certain types of church organizations skew the data so as to produce the overall negative result.

Analysis of Employee Responses

A close sociological analysis of the employee data turned up no significant differences when considering the respondents' gender, education, or length of employment. Analyzing the employee data by type of employer revealed some interesting differences. As indicated earlier, only 40% of employees felt that they would receive just treatment during a grievance. Employees in diocesan employment reflected the national average exactly, while a somewhat lower percentage of parish employees and higher percentage of religious congregation employees felt they would receive just treatment. Table 1 displays both the positive and the negative views expressed in the survey.

TABLE 1
All Employee Responses Analyzed by Type of Employer

Analysis of employees responding to "If I have a legitimate grievance about working conditions, the church will treat me justly."				
Response Category	National Data For all employees	Data by Type of Employer		
		Parish	Diocese	Religious Congregation
Agree: Will Receive Just Treatment	40%	37%	40%	48%
Disagree: Will Not Receive Just Treatment	30%	32%	30%	19%

Analysis of employee opinion in these workplaces by employee status (priest, religious or lay) revealed additional interesting findings. First, the relatively high ranking received by religious congregation workplaces was not caused solely by the responses of religious, as might be expected, but also by the positive responses of their lay employees. Lay employees exhibited little difference whether they worked for parishes or dioceses but those that worked for religious congregations felt significantly better about just treatment during a grievance. Table 2 illustrates this point.

Religious employees also exhibited significantly different response rates by type of employer. Religious employed by dioceses felt most likely to receive just treatment during a grievance—a 55% agree-

TABLE 2
Lay Employee Responses Analyzed by Type of Employer

Analysis of lay employees responding to "If I have a legitimate grievance about working conditions, the church will treat me justly."					
Response Category	National Data For All Employees	National Data For Lay Employees	Data by Type of Employer		
			Parish	Diocese	Religious Congregation
Agree: Will Receive Just Treatment	40%	37%	37%	34%	48%
Disagree: Will Not Receive Just Treatment	30%	33%	34%	33%	24%

ment rate. Religious employed by parishes felt least likely to receive just treatment. These findings are displayed in Table 3.

TABLE 3
Religious Responses Analyzed by Type of Employer

Analysis of religious employees responding to "If I have a legitimate grievance about working conditions, the church will treat me justly."					
Response Category	National Data Employees	National Data For Religious Employees	Data by Type of Employer		
			Parish	Diocese	Religious Congregation
Agree: Will Receive Just Treatment	40%	46%	33%	55%	46%
Disagree: Will Not Receive Just Treatment	30%	23%	31%	21%	15%

The positive responses of diocesan priests at 44% was somewhat higher than the national average but did not differ when analyzed by where they were working—in a parish or diocesan setting. None reported working for a religious congregation.

The following conclusions emerged when all these data were combined. The religious congregation workplace surfaced as most likely to provide just treatment during a grievance. While receiving higher ratings than other employer types, however, religious congregations still need to improve since fewer than half their employees held that opinion. Religious employees provided the other interesting departure from the norm. Over half (55%) of religious working for dioceses felt they would be treated justly during a grievance. This differed substantially from the opinion of lay employees working for dioceses (34% agreement) and religious working for parishes (33% agreement).

Characteristics of Workplaces With Low Just Treatment Expectations

The NACPA survey included several items closely related to the question of receiving just treatment during a grievance. Analysis of these questions provided some insight into the types of church workplaces where employees perceive grievances will be handled fairly. The first question is most directly related. It asks about employee comfort level in discussing difficulties and differences of opinion with supervisors. Two other questions cover basic communication devices about work expectations, job descriptions and performance evaluations. The last question investigates participation in decision making over working conditions.

TABLE 4
Correlation of Attitude about Just Treatment during a Grievance with Questions on Related Personnel Practices

Questions about Related Personnel Practices	Positive Correlation Percentage of respondents agreeing with related statements who also anticipate just treatment during a grievance	Negative Correlation Percentage of respondents disagreeing with statements who also do not anticipate just treatment during a grievance
	Completely Agree	*Completely Disagree*
Free to discuss problems with supervisor	61%	75%
Have a clear Job description	52%	62%
Receive annual performance evaluations	55%	41%
Participate in decision making	63%	72%

In general, both administrator and employee expectations of grievance just treatment were significantly related to responses to these questions. Employee responses displayed a high positive correlation and an even higher negative correlation on these items. This indicates that workplaces lacking some or all of these—good communication with supervisor, job descriptions, performance evaluations, and participation in decision-making are those most likely to employ workers with negative expectations about just treatment during grievances. Table 4 substantiates this conclusion.

This data was analyzed further to determine if any particular employee groups or types of workplace showed a significant correlation between these questions and expectations of just treatment during grievances. Earlier, religious congregation workplaces proved to have

TABLE 5
Responses to Questions About Closely Related Personnel Practices
by Type of Organization

Closely Related Statement in Data	Employee responses agreeing or completely agreeing to the related statements analyzed by type of church organization		
	Parish	Diocese	Religious Congregation
Free to discuss problems with supervisors	73%	69%	81%
Have a clear job description	72%	72%	83%
Receive annual performance evaluation	38%	53%	69%
Participate in decision making	71%	73%	76%

the highest percentage of employees with positive perceptions of the grievance process. The data on closely related personnel practices is consistent with that finding. As Table 5 shows, religious congregation workplaces consistently rate higher on the application of these procedures.

Analysis of Administrator Responses

Further inspection of the administrator responses to the survey reveal some interesting patterns. There were no significant differences in responses among administrators based on education, field, length of employment and age. Differences do exist based on gender, status and employer. Women administrators were less likely to expect that employees would receive just treatment during a grievance. Specifically, 49% of men administrators and only 33% of women administrators expected employees to receive just treatment.

Administrators in diocesan settings were also more likely to expect just treatment to occur while administrators for religious congregations were less likely. Specifically while 42% of all administrators expected employees to receive just treatment during grievances, 46% of diocesan administrators and only 34% of administrators at religious congregation complexes held this expectation.

Further analysis revealed significant differences among lay, religious, and priest administrators at these workplaces. The low evaluation by religious congregation administrators was due primarily to religious, who agreed only 33% of the time that just treatment would occur in their workplace during a grievance. Lay administrators at religious congregations, on the other hand, exhibited a 55% agreement rate. The relatively high ranking of their workplace by diocesan administrators was due primarily to priests who evaluated their grievance processes positively 57% of the time. The response rates of religious and lay administrators in dioceses were similarly lower, with 38% and 40% respectively expressing positive views about their grievance procedures. The administrator evaluations of both workplaces are displayed in the following table.

TABLE 6
Administrator Responses Analyzed by Type of Employer and State in Life

Analysis of administrators responding to "If employees have a legitimate grievance about working conditions, the church will treat them justly."						
Response Category	National Data for Administrators	Data by Type of Employer and State in Life				
		Diocesan Workplaces			Congregation Workplaces	
		Priest	Religious	Lay	Religious	Lay
Agree: Will Receive Just Treatment	42%	57%	38%	40%	33%	55%
Disagree: Will Not Receive	25%	8%	33%	34%	30%	22%

IMPLICATIONS AND OBSERVATIONS

The sociological analysis of the data suggests that grievances are processed most justly in religious congregation workplaces and for religious employees in dioceses. None of these findings, however, produce an overwhelmingly positive picture of grievance handling by church organizations. What lies behind this negative impression? Is it possible to identify some of the reasons for such a low perception of church grievance processes?

EXISTENCE OF GRIEVANCE PROCEDURES

An obvious place to look first is at the existence and structure of grievance procedures in church workplaces. Do procedures exist at all?

If so, are they clearly delineated and communicated? Are they structured to facilitate constructive solutions and build high morale?

Structure of Grievance Procedures

Another consideration concerns structure. Do the procedures contain the elements necessary for effective grievance handling? To be successful, grievance procedures should exhibit a number of characteristics similar to those displayed in Table 7.[1]

Table 7. Elements of Effective Grievance Resolution Procedures

1. A clear and fully articulated procedure
2. Access to the grievance procedure as an employee right
3. Absense of reprisal against those filing grievances
4. A simple, easy to use procedure
5. A procedure encouraging resolution at the earliest stages
6. Assistance available to employee complainants
7. Assistance to supervisors faced with a complaint
8. A process that preserves confidentiality
9. Timely decisions guaranteed through timetables
10. Decision makers free to ask any question, obtain all facts
11. Decision makers independent of management control

When organizations omit no reprisal guarantees, early resolution processes, assistance to grievants and timetables which assure continued processing all the way to resolution, employees understandably perceive the process as unfriendly and ineffective.

The grievance process should include a no reprisal clause, assistance to employees, and the protection of confidentiality. Assuming that decision makers are free of management control is difficult to implement because it represents a significant departure from current practice for most church organizations. Yet the fact that some church organizations have introduced this feature into their procedures suggest that it is not entirely alien to the church environment.

CHALLENGES

Much effort needs to be made by church employers to improve the perception of workers about grievance handling in church workplaces. The findings from this study suggest productive courses to pursue. It will be important to encourage personnel practices which enhance communication between employees and supervisors. In the survey, workplaces with such practices received high ratings for fair handling of grievances. Improvement of church grievance procedures is also needed.

To achieve these goals, it is clear that certain key issues need lengthy discussion. The grievance decision-making process is one. Grievance decision making free of management control is a most important ingredient in an effective grievance procedure. But adopting it appears to involve a sharing of power with employees. This can be a difficult prospect for organizations. Yet, some church organizations have established grievance procedures in which final decision making is free of management control. And some of the most effective companies in the nation incorporate this component of workplace justice into their procedures. Efforts need to be made to demonstrate how this apparent giving up of power enhances organizational power.

Another key issue involves developing ways to enhance workplace communication to minimize the need to process formal grievances. Many workplace problems are resolved by simple communication between employee and supervisor. Sage advice from past experience may facilitate resolution. Discussion with peers can increase objectivity. The Human Resource Office may be able to mediate conflict by providing a better understanding of policies.

CONCLUSION

Responding to both of these key issues, improving communications and establishing or improving grievance procedures, will do much to alter not only the perceptions of employees about just treatment but also the reality of just treatment in the workplace.

— *9* —

Compensation

by

Colleen Branagan, MS

Perhaps the most basic and universal understanding about work is that those who work will receive recompense in exchange for the goods or services they provide. The method and type of compensation has varied significantly throughout time and cultures. Bartering was one of the earliest forms of compensation. Long before money/currency existed, people exchanged their talents, goods, or services for other talents, goods, services or rewards. Today, compensation may be defined as all forms of financial returns, tangible services, and benefits employees receive as part of an employment relationship. (Milkovich, 1990).

In this last decade of the 20th century, American employers, no matter how large or small, recognize the importance of developing compensation "packages" that can attract and retain competent, committed employees. Employers know that compensation is a critical part of the equation in achieving their ultimate bottom line—a positive "return on investment." Human resource directors understand compensation to include a variety of direct and indirect financial costs, goods, and services. Compensation may be received directly in the form of cash, such as salaries, wages, stipends, or merit raises/bonuses. It is also indirectly received through benefits such as FICA contributions; pensions; medical, dental, and disability insurance; paid holidays, retreats, vacation, and sick leave; housing/car allowances; tuition reimbursement, etc. (Milkovich, 1990:4-5).

In addition to these direct and indirect forms of compensation, there are other ways in which employees can be rewarded by working for an organization. These are sometimes less easy to quantify, and until fairly recently, were not typically considered as part of a total compensation package.

They include such things as: a safe, healthy environment; quality of supervision; participation in decision-making about issues affecting the work life; personal commitment to the nature or purpose of the organization; promotional opportunities; flex-time; job security; geographical location. In church organizations, there is also the inherent potential for employees to connect directly their faith and work life. Although these kinds of intrinsic rewards are difficult to measure in dollars, they are nonetheless a significant addition to the total compensation "package" that employers can offer.

HISTORY

The Church As Employer in the United States

The Catholic Church is one of the oldest employers in the United States. Some of the earliest hospitals, schools, and charitable organizations were church or church-related organizations. Hundreds and thousands of parishes were established. Large numbers of workers staffed these organizations. However, for over 200 years, the primary work force in these organizations (excluding hospitals), were vowed religious, clergy, or lay volunteers. For the religious and clergy, compensation was primarily a form of bartering. Little if any "currency" was exchanged; in return for dedicating their life to the church, their room and board and other basic "temporal" needs were provided, sometimes only after persistent and creative prompting.

In a recent study of Catholic Church lay pension plans (Diocesan Lay Retirement Systems, 1988), it was extrapolated that there are at least 250,000 people who are compensated for work from the Catholic Church or church-sponsored organizations throughout the United States. At least 85% of those are paid lay employees. In only 25 years, the demographic characteristics of the church's work force has dramatically changed. One of the most obvious and significant implications of this change is the need to develop compensation packages that are just, competitive, and affordable.

The Church's Social Teachings about Just Compensation

In 1891, Pope Leo XIII's *Rerum Novarum* encyclical represented the first of a number of magisterial teachings on the just treatment of workers.

His writings were directed to the "secular" employers, and did not reflect on the church as an employer. This encyclical addresses such topics as the dignity of labor and the right of working persons to form associations. It defines just remuneration as being enough to "support the wage earner in reasonable and frugal comfort." (Just Treatment, 1986:15)

In 1971 Pope Paul VI's *Octogesima Adveniens* states that every man (sic) has the right to work and to equitable remuneration which will enable him and his family to "lead a worthy life from the material, social, cultural, and spiritual level and to (receive) assistance in the case of need arising from sickness or age." (Just Treatment, 1986:16)

In 1990, the National Conference of Diocesan Directors published a report entitled "Just Wages and Benefits for Lay and Religious Church Employees." In it, a synthesis of the church's teachings on just compensation is offered:

> Catholic social teachings on the just treatment of employees flows from the dignity of the human person, a dignity that can only be realized in community. This teaching holds that the rights for workers include: just remuneration (that enables a household to live in dignity, taking into account local cultural and social development); . . . adequate health care; sufficient period of rest and leisure; security for unemployment, disability and retirement (pension); healthful working conditions . . . self-development and participation in decision-making. (Just Wages and Benefits, 1990:2.)

FINDINGS OF THE SURVEY ON COMPENSATION

One of the components of the survey asked Catholic Church employees, administrators and Catholics in general to assess the adequacy of compensation paid to church workers. It is important to note that the term "compensation" was *not* defined; it is impossible, therefore, to know just what the respondents meant when they answered questions about compensation.

The questions were different for administrators (those workers with supervisory responsibilities) than for employees (professional and support staff). The administrators were asked to rate the adequacy of compensation for church workers in general, while the employees were asked to rate the adequacy of their own compensation.

There were three general questions related to compensation.

I. How do you rate the compensation that church workers are now receiving for their work in terms of being able to meet their own personal needs?

Responses were as follows:

	Employees Rate Own Pay	Admin. Rate All Workers	Laity Rate All Workers
Good - Excellent	44%	27%	21%
Fair - Poor	55%	72%	66%
No opinion		13%	

It is interesting that 44% of the employees ranked their own compensation as excellent or good, while only 27% of the administrators rated compensation for all church workers as excellent or good. Also only 21% of the laity in general believed that church workers' compensation is at least good.

Other Demographic Characteristics

For the church employees surveyed, their overall responses can be broken down further by looking at such demographic characteristics as status, gender, and place of employment.

Specifically, 63% of single persons and 76% of single parents rated their compensation fair-poor; 69% of married persons with no children and 60% of married persons with children rated their compensation fair-poor; 43% of religious rated their compensation fair-poor; 45% of diocesan priests rated their compensation fair-poor.

When the data is compared by gender, nearly 12% of men reported their compensation as excellent and less than 5% of women reported their compensation as excellent; about 50% of men reported their compensation as fair-poor; about 60% of women reported their compensation as fair-poor.

Finally, no significant relationship appeared between the employees' rating of their compensation and whether they worked at a parish, a diocese, or a religious congregation (See Table 1).

II. How do you rate the compensation church workers are now receiving for their work in terms of being able to meet family or congregational family needs?

	Employees Rate Own Pay	Admin. Rate All Workers	Laity Rate All Workers
Good - Excellent	34%	19%	16%
Fair - Poor	63%	79%	67%
No opinion		18%	

Other Demographic Characteristics

As might be expected, a greater number of all types of employees rated their compensation as less able to meet family/congregational family needs than their own personal needs.

According to status, 65% of single persons and 84% of single parents rated their compensation fair-poor; 76% of married workers with no children and 69% of married persons with children rated their compensation as fair-poor; 56% of religious rated their compensation as fair-poor; 57% of diocesan priests rated their compensation as fair-poor.

Following the same pattern, according to gender about 8% of all male employees rated their compensation excellent; less than 3% of

TABLE 1
Adequacy of Compensation for Personal Needs Rated
Fair-Poor by Employees

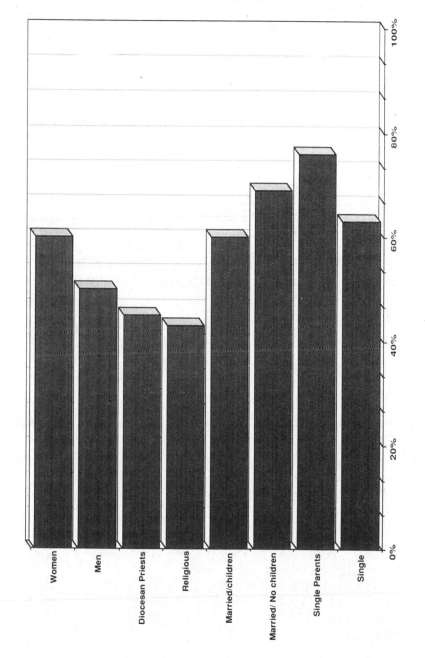

female employees rated their compensation excellent; about 60% of male employees rated their compensation fair-poor; nearly 69% of female employees rated their compensation fair-poor.

Again, there was not a significant relationship between where employees were employed and their rating of compensation for family needs (See Table 2).

III. How do you rate the compensation church workers now receive in comparison to what other workers in the area receive?

	Employees Rate Own Pay	Admin. Rate All Workers	Laity Rate All Workers
Good - Excellent	25%	14%	n/a
Fair - Poor	74%	83%	n/a

It is perhaps not surprising that an overwhelming majority of all employees surveyed believed they do not compare positively to what other workers in their area receive for compensation. For example, 71% of single persons and 96% of single parents rated their compensation as fair-poor; 76% of married persons with no children and 75% of married persons with children rated their compensation as fair-poor; 75% of religious rated their compensation as fair-poor; 71% of diocesan priests rated their compensation as fair-poor.

When compared by gender, about 5% of male employees rated their salary as excellent; 2% of female employees rated their salary as excellent; nearly 68% of male employees rated their salary as fair-poor; about 79% of female employees rated their salary as fair-poor.

ADDITIONAL FINDINGS REGARDING ADEQUACY OF COMPENSATION

Employees' ratings of whether their compensation was adequate was also significantly correlated to questions relating to:

1. Whether the employee was thinking of finding a position elsewhere (those who were thinking of finding another position were more likely to rate their compensation as fair-poor);

2. Whether the employee believed he/she could easily find another job (those who thought they could easily find another job were more likely to say their current salary was only fair or poor);

3. Whether the employee thought he/she might some day be unable to afford to work for the church (those who might some day be unable to afford to work for the church were more likely to rate their compensation as fair-poor); and

TABLE 2
Adequacy of Compensation for Personal Needs Rated
Fair-Poor by Employees

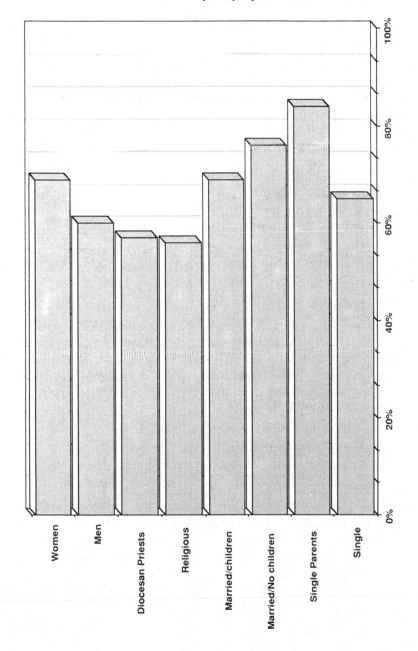

4. Whether the employee was willing to sacrifice to work for the church (those who rated their salaries as good-excellent were more likely to say they were willing to make financial sacrifices).

BENEFITS

In addition to salaries, wages, or stipends, the second component of compensation is benefits. The NACPA Survey asked administrators and employees to rate the benefits church workers receive from the parish, diocese, or religious congregation in which they work. Administrators rated benefits for all workers while employees rated their own benefits; 8% of the employees were part time. These benefits included:

Health Care/Health Insurance
Retirement Plan
Disability Insurance
Life Insurance
Reimbursement for education expenses
Paid Vacations
Paid Holidays

HEALTH CARE

A majority of both church administrators (66%) and church employees (58%) gave either good or excellent ratings to the health care/insurance benefits currently provided by their employer. However, 58 (9%) of the employees surveyed indicated their employer provided NO health care/insurance. Of those 58, 49 were lay employees, 9 were religious and 1 was a priest.

RETIREMENT PLAN

About one-third of both the administrators and employees rated their retirement plan as good or excellent; however, 4% of the administrators and 11% of the employees reported their employer provides NO retirement plan. About 68% of those reporting they were not on a retirement plan were lay employees; 31% were religious and 1% were priests. Finally, of those that reported no retirement plan, 75% were female and 25% were male.

The survey also asked church administrators and employees whether lay church members in their area believe the church provides generous retirement and working benefits to its workers. About 23% of administrators and 32% of employees believed lay church members think the church provides generous retirement and working benefits to employees. When laity themselves were sampled, over 40% couldn't answer the question because they didn't know what the retirement policies/practices were; however, about 28% of those sampled indicated they believed the church provides generous retirement and working benefits.

DISABILITY INSURANCE

About one in three administrators and employees gave positive ratings to the disability insurance provided by their employers. However, 19% of the administrators and 29% of all employees reported they had NO disability insurance coverage. Interestingly, although religious comprised 21% of the employees surveyed, 30% of those reporting no disability insurance were members of religious communities.

LIFE INSURANCE

This is not a highly "visible" benefit; it is sometimes included as part of the disability insurance plan. Although one quarter of both administrators and employees rated their life insurance plan as good or excellent, 24% of administrators and 34% of employees reported their employer did not provide this benefit at all. Although only 14% of the employees surveyed were priests, 41% of the priests reported having no life insurance provided; 54% of religious surveyed had no life insurance. About one in four lay employees did not have life insurance. Clearly, life insurance has not received significant attention as a benefit particularly for priests or religious.

REIMBURSEMENT FOR EDUCATIONAL EXPENSES

About one in five administrators rated their employers' policy or practice of reimbursing for educational expenses as good or excellent. Interestingly, a higher percentage (31%) of employees thought so. This fact becomes more understandable when the respondents are compared by status. For example, 48% of all priests surveyed rated reimbursement practices as good or excellent, while 27% of lay employees and 31% of religious employees thought so. However, 19% of administrators and 30% of employees reported there was no reimbursement for educational expenses. Of those employees reporting no reimbursement, 74% are lay employees, 23% are religious, and 4% are priests.

PAID VACATIONS

This benefit received very positive ratings from both administrators and workers. About two-thirds of both groups rated this benefit as good or excellent, although 4% of administrators and 10% of employees (69) reported they did not get paid vacations. This group of 69 employees reporting no paid vacation included 45 lay employees, 17 religious, and 7 priests.

PAID HOLIDAYS

As with the ratings for paid vacations, both church administrators and employees gave very positive ratings to this benefit. About 70% of both groups rated their employers' paid holiday policy or practice as good or excellent; again a small number of administrators (3%) and a higher number of employees (10%) reported they did not receive paid holidays.

The survey also asked the sample of Catholic laity their perceptions of the quality of benefits received by church administrators and employees.

Their answers were as follows: about one lay person in five apparently had no knowledge of the benefits received by workers for the church. Among those giving ratings, relatively fewer gave positive ratings to health care insurance (41%), paid vacations (30%) or paid holidays (32%) than they assume are received by the workers. Their ratings of the other benefits are about the same as those given by the administrators and employees (See Table 3).

SUMMARY OF BENEFITS SURVEY

It is in the area of providing benefits that the church as employer scores the highest ratings. Whereas fewer than 25% of administrators and employees viewed their (salary) compensation as good to excellent, about 65% of those two groups rated the significant benefits of pension, health care, paid vacation and holidays as good to excellent.

The other significant benefit on the survey reimbursement for educational expenses appears to be the one benefit which does not exist for many administrators (18%) and employees (30%), especially if that administrator or worker is a lay employee. Additionally, this benefit, if provided at all, is rated fair or poor by a majority of the administrators and 35% of the employees.

TABLE 3
Rating of Benefits as Good or Excellent

JOB SECURITY

Attitudes of administrators and employees about job security was another subject the NACPA survey addressed. In this section, administrators were asked to rate how they believe the employees they supervise feel about five questions that relate to the notion of job security. Likewise, employees were asked to rate their own feelings about the same five issues.

The questions were as follows:

1. How secure do you (or the employees you supervise) feel about your long-term future with the church?

In general, employees felt more secure about their futures than their administrators presumed they did. About three in four employees said they are at least fairly secure about their long-term future with the church compared with 60% of the administrators who believed employees have this level of confidence. Only 5% of employees reported they were "not at all secure." Of that 5%, 87% were lay employees.

Although a majority of all church workers said they are at least fairly secure, it is interesting to segregate the number and type of workers who felt "very" secure about their long-term future as a church worker. About 32% of all employees surveyed reported this highest level of security. However, of that group, only 22% of all lay employees felt this way, while 66% of priests and 42% of all religious felt very secure. Such information is not particularly surprising, given the nature of the lifetime commitment by priests and religious.

2. How secure would you (or the employees you supervise) feel if the leadership of the parish or diocese changes?

In this case, about 44% of the administrators believed the employees they supervise feel fairly secure and 65% of the employees felt at least fairly secure should there be a major leadership change. This difference may be explained in that administrators may be projecting their own feelings about job security should there be a change in parish/diocesan leadership. Since 71% of the administrators are priests or religious, many of them are directly appointed by the (Arch)bishop or pastor to a particular position. Their tenure in their current job/assignment is sometimes directly dependent upon the current leader. However, even if their ability to retain their current position is less possible should there be a change in leadership, they still have job security. That is to say, priests may be reassigned or placed elsewhere within the church's organizational structure; they would not, however, need to look for employment outside of the church.

This observation is born out when looking more carefully at the characteristics of all employees who reported feeling "very" secure should there be a change in leadership. Nearly 32% of all priests felt very secure, while only 10% of lay employees and 18% of religious felt that way.

3. How secure would you (or your employees) feel if your immediate supervisor changed?

Answers to this question proved similar in pattern to the previous question. In this case, about 56% of administrators believed their employees would feel at least fairly secure about retaining their job should the immediate supervisor change; 72% of the employees felt that way. Only 7% of the employees surveyed felt not at all secure in their job should their immediate supervisor change; 4% of those are priests and 65% are lay employees. Again, administrators believed their employees would be more apprehensive about changes than the employees themselves reported.

4. How well do you (or the employees you supervise) feel you would be provided for if you became incapacitated and could no longer work?

In this case, a majority of employees (57%) felt insecure about being (financially) provided for; 65% of the administrators believed their employees feel insecure about this issue. Of those that reported "Not at All Secure," 31% were women and 19% were men; 84% were lay employees, 3% were priests, and 13% were religious.

It is worth comparing this information with the data regarding disability insurance. Over 60% of all employees reported their disability insurance plan was fair, poor, or non-existent. It is probably not surprising then, that 57% of those same employees felt "insecure" about being provided for should they become incapacitated.

Finally, although 64% of lay employees, 37% of priests, and 61% of religious regarded their disability plan as fair, poor, or non-existent, 84% of lay employees, 3% of priests, and 13% of religious felt not at all secure about being provided for should they become incapacitated. It may be surmised from this comparison that lay employees do not see the church as a realistic resource should they become incapacitated, but priests and religious do.

5. How well do you (or the employees you supervise) feel you will be provided for in your retirement years?

A majority (58%) of all employees surveyed did not feel secure about being adequately provided for in their retirement years. Within that group are 70% of all lay employees surveyed, 36% of all priests, and 39% of all religious. A majority of administrators also believed their employees were apprehensive about adequate retirement.

It is helpful to look at the results of this question in comparison to the question regarding the adequacy of the current retirement plan provided by the employer. Over 65% of all employees surveyed reported their current retirement plan was fair, poor, or non-existent. Of that 65%, 72% were lay employees, 11% were priests, and 17% were religious.

CHALLENGES

The results of this attitudinal survey indicated a number of challenges the church as an employer needs to address.

1. The majority of church administrators and employees felt their compensation is not adequate to meet their personal or familial (congregational) needs.

Strategic responses to this challenge certainly include reviewing/revising a parish, diocese, or religious congregation's current revenues and expenses. On the revenue side, many parishes, dioceses and religious congregations are not as effective as they must be in raising funds to support the cost of providing adequate salaries and benefits.

2. Many of the church administrators and employees gave positive ratings to most of the benefits provided by their employer.

It is in this area of compensation that the church is most competitive. For those parishes, dioceses, or religious congregations that do not yet provide basic health care and/or retirement plans, this must be a high priority.

One of the challenges the church as an employer needs to recognize is that it must compete in the secular marketplace for employees. Parishes, schools, and dioceses need to recruit, screen, select, and retain excellent workers. Part of a successful recruitment and selection process involves the parish, diocese, school being able to tell (and sell) potential employees about the unique, attractive, and inviting aspects of the worklife. This certainly includes a just, competitive compensation package. Although the church has a way to go in providing competitive salaries and wages, it has made significant strides in providing competitive benefits.

3. In responding to questions regarding job security, a majority of employees felt fairly secure about retaining their job should leadership or their supervisor change in their parish, diocese, or religious congregation.

The "downside" of job security occurs when workers are not free to leave their current job or place of work. Because of the nature of their relationship with the bishop or religious community, some measure of this freedom to leave is given up. That is not to say that lay employees should appreciate this freedom to terminate employment; it is simply to round out the full context of what the implications of job security can also mean.

A challenge for church organizations is to respond to church workers regarding the need for job security. One way to do this is to provide financial assistance to those who may lose jobs as a result of leadership transitions. For those who lose their jobs due to retirement, or accidents/illness, it is appropriate to develop and maintain adequate pension, workers compensation, and disability plans.

4. The scope of this attitudinal survey did not substantially cover the third aspect of compensation that was identified at the beginning of this article. These are the less quantifiable, intrinsic benefits or rewards of working for a parish, diocese, or other church organization. It is in this area that there exists a particularly rich potential for the Catholic Church as employer to create and maintain a just, healthy, and competitive workplace.

5. In analyzing the data, some of the different needs, expectations, and attitudes of priests, religious and lay employees became apparent. As a next step, it might also be valuable for the church to compare the attitudes of current church workers with workers from other public, private, and non-profit organizations. It could then be known how the church compares both internally and externally as an employer.

CONCLUSION

Although the Catholic Church is one of the oldest employers, it is only in the last part of the 20th century that the church has begun a conscious, systematic approach to defining the employment relationship between itself and the thousands of church workers. People who work for the church expect and deserve just and competitive compensation. Parishes, dioceses, and religious congregations must begin and/or continue to develop and implement comprehensive compensation policies and practices for all those who work for the church.

— *10* —

Affirmative Action
by
Francis Kelly Scheets, OSC, Ph.D.

HISTORICAL PERSPECTIVE

Throughout the history of Catholicism people who were responsible for fulfilling the mission of the church were priests, sisters and brothers who dedicated their lives to this work. In return, they were sustained and compensated by their religious congregations, dioceses, or church institutions. The church, through these religious congregations and diocesan systems, undertook what today may be considered classic personnel functions, i.e. recruiting, selecting, training, compensating, and supporting its employees.

Dramatic and fundamental changes have been experienced by the church in the past twenty-five years.

In 1971 the National Association of Church Personnel Administrators (NACPA) was founded. The mission is "to identify skills and competencies for human resource managers, develop personnel systems which integrate management and pastoral values, and advocate standards of just treatments for church personnel." This purpose statement recognizes that "a comprehensive approach to personnel concerns of *all* people working for the church must be the foundation for the development of policies and procedures."

FINDINGS OF THE SURVEY ON AFFIRMATIVE ACTION

The NACPA Survey conducted by Gallup contained these questions:

8. How do you rate the church in your area for its record in recruiting and hiring people from the following group? (Rec-

ognizing of course that exceptions must be made sometimes because a position requires Catholic Church membership, ordinations, etc.) *Women, Blacks, Other minorities, Disabled Persons, Young people, People over 50*

9. How do you rate the church for its record in promoting people from these groups? *Women, Blacks, Other minorities, Disabled persons*

RECRUITMENT AND HIRING AND PROMOTION

In order to fully understand some of the responses it would help to know that women and lay workers were disproportionately concentrated in dead-end staff positions within the church. (La Magdeleine, 1986:323 and Rosenberg and Sullivan, 1980:75) Priests held 64% of the top nineteen diocesan positions in the church; lay men held 18%, mostly in finance and administration. Women (religious and lay) held but 16%, concentrated in the typically "female" areas of schools and religious education. (*Conscience*, 1988:6)

The NACPA survey clearly showed that women and administrators were more likely than men to value promotion opportunities, and women administrators were more dissatisfied with the promotion opportunities provided by the church.

The church's record for recruiting and hiring women received good marks ("excellent" to "good") from administrators (82%) and employees (83%). Male administrators rated the record high (93%), whereas fewer female administrators gave it a high rating (70%). The record for promotion was not quite as good; 60% of administrators and 58% of employees gave the church good marks.

Dramatically fewer administrators (26%) and employees (37%) gave the local church "excellent" to "good" marks for the recruitment and hiring of Blacks. Again, it was the male administrator who gave the church a slightly better rating (30%) than did the female administrator (21%). When it came to promotion of Blacks, both the administrators (30%) and the employees (37%) felt the church had managed "excellent" to "good."

Regarding the recruitment and hiring of all other minorities, 32% of the administrators and 42% of employees gave the church a good rating. Only one-in-three of administrators (32%) and employees (39%) felt the church had done reasonably well in promoting other minorities.

Less than one-fifth of the administrators (19%) and one-third of employees (30%) thought the church did well in recruiting and hiring persons with disabilities. The same percentages held in assessing promotions for persons with disabilities: administrators (21%) and employees (30%).

Figure 1.
Administrators' Assessment of Church Affirmation Action in Recruit-ing and Hiring
(Hiring Evaluation: Excellent to Good)

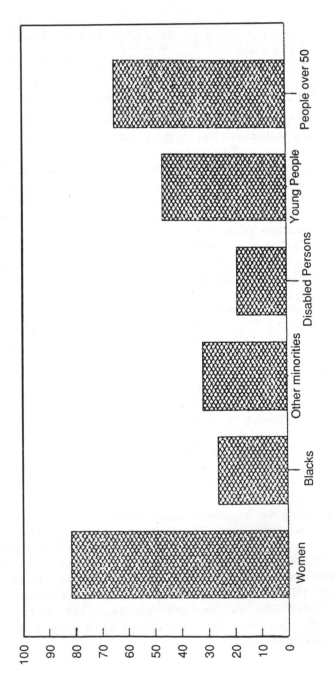

Two-in-three administrators (65%) and employees (60%) said that the church has done well in recruiting and hiring people over 50 who may be looking for a second career. Typically male administrators were high (72%) in evaluating the church, while fewer female administrators (59%) agreed. In the recruitment and hiring of young people (those under 35 years of age) less than half the administrators (46%) and employees (50%) believed the church had done well.

In general, employees agreed with the administrators; however, they gave slightly higher marks (37%) to the church for the recruitment and hiring of Blacks and persons with disabilities.

Figure 1 above shows that administrators were very satisfied with the current policies and practices regarding the hiring of women and somewhat satisfied with the hiring of people over 50 who are considering a second career.

However a poor third gave "excellent" to "good" marks for the hiring of Blacks, other minorities, and persons with disabilities.

Administrators were less satisfied with the promotion of women (60%) in the church and many were concerned about the church's practice in promoting Blacks, other minorities and persons with disabilities.

FACTORS INFLUENCING EVALUATIONS

Male And Female Administrators

A significant difference occurs when the "excellent" to "good" evaluations given by male administrators are compared with those given by female administrators. Table 1 notes the areas where the difference is greater than ten percentage points. With the exception of the recruitment and hiring of Blacks and the hiring and promotion of persons with disabilities, female administrators differed in their evaluations from the male administrators by more than ten negative percentage points (-10%) in many areas. Figure 2 illustrates the magnitude of difference.

TABLE 1
Level of Satisfaction Statements and Scores
and Administrators

Satisfaction Statements	Percent Very Satisfied	
	Male	Female
My involvement with ministry	65%	55%
The responsibility I have been given	73%	64%
The recognition I receive from my work	46%	47%
Average	61%	55%

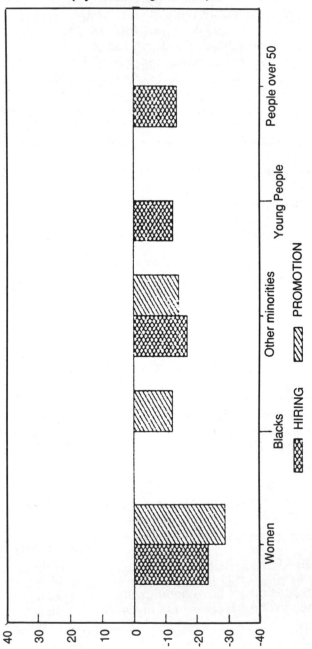

Figure 2
Variation of Female From Male Administrators in Assessment of
Church Affirmative Action
(By Percentage Points)

The strongest disagreements were with the hiring (-23%) and promotion (-29%) of women. Female administrators did not strongly disagree over the recruitment and hiring of Blacks but did so regarding their promotion (-12%). They also differed significantly in the hiring (-17%) and promotion (-14%) of other minorities. They likewise differed with male administrators over the hiring of young people under 35 years of age (-12%) and of those over 50 years (-14%).

Female employees did not differ from their male counterparts by more than ten percentage points regarding the recruitment and hiring of Blacks and persons with disabilities. However, these wide variations among the administrators need to be explored further.

Factor Analysis

Factor analysis of the data indicated that three sets of statements had a significant relationship as to how an administrator evaluated affirmative action in the church regarding recruitment, hiring, and promotion: the level of education,[1] the level of satisfaction,[2] and the Scale of Dissatisfaction.[3]

The survey did not identify the ethnic or racial background of the respondents, nor did it identify those who were handicapped. For that reason these qualifications were not matter for factor analysis.

Education

Administrators were very well educated. Post graduate degrees were common for both male (81%) and female (83%) administrators.

Education level had an *inverse* impact of how administrators evaluated the church's record in recruiting and hiring Blacks, other minorities and the disabled. In other words, the better educated the administrator the greater the chance that he or she would respond with "fair" to "poor" scores. Education had no significant impact on the perceptions about hiring and promoting young persons (under 35) and people over 50.

The level of education received had no effect on the administrators' estimation of the church's affirmative action record in regard to women. The education of administrators had an *inverse* effect as to how they evaluated hiring persons with disabilities; but it had a *direct* impact on how their promotion was perceived.

In summation it can be noted that better educated administrators indicated that the church has only a "fair" to "poor" record in recruiting and hiring Blacks; but it has a much better record in hiring and promoting of women, young persons and people over 50 years.

Level of Satisfaction

Three statements used to determine the "level of satisfaction" were rated "very satisfied" by about the same percent of men and women.

On average 59% of all administrators were "very satisfied" to "somewhat satisfied" regarding their ministry involvement, responsibility, and recognition received. (There was a slight difference in the average level of satisfaction scores between male (61%) and female (55%) administrators, with females a bit less satisfied.)[4] Table 1 shows that there was a wide variation among the three statements. While most administrators are very satisfied with the responsibility received, there is not much "enthusiasm" shown for the recognition received as less than half of both male and female administrators were very satisfied.

Satisfaction had a *direct* impact on how administrators evaluated the church's current position on the recruitment and hiring and promotion of Blacks and the hiring of other minorities. Strangely, the satisfaction level had an *inverse* effect on the hiring of persons with disabilities, but a *direct* effect on their promotion. There was no effect on the hiring of persons over 50 but a *direct* effect on the hiring of young persons.

The satisfaction experienced by administrators had a direct influence on the "excellent" to "good" ratings given to the church's hiring and promotion of women.

In summation the following can be noted: Those administrators who were satisfied tended to give the church marks of "excellent" to "good"; those who were dissatisfied tended to give the church marks of "fair" to "poor."

Scale of Dissatisfaction

Seven survey questions indicated a marked degree of "dissatisfaction" among female administrators. The response for statements 1 through 5 was "Agree Completely" and "Very True" for 6 and 7.

1) The restrictive rules of the church deny the opportunity to grow and work to my ability.

2) Many persons object to the church's stand on the treatment of women.

3) Clergy are reluctant to share their duties.

4) Lay workers do not get enough recognition for their work.

5) Unless some church policies become more open I may cease working for the church.

6) No matter how much I disagree, I must always submit to the will and teachings of the church.

On the average 41% of the administrators "completely agreed" or "agreed" with the Scale of Dissatisfaction statements. However there was a marked difference between the average level of dissatisfaction for male (37%) and female (52%) administrators.[5] Those who placed high on this scale tended to have an *inverse* effect on the evaluation of the church's record on recruitment, hiring and promotion of Blacks, minorities, disabled, young, older persons, and women. This dissatisfaction scale was a strong predictor for "fair" to "poor" scores on the affirmative action issues under consideration.

In other words, the dissatisfaction variables were consistent predictors of an administrator's evaluation (or even an employee's) of the church's record in hiring and promoting minorities.

MALE AND FEMALE EMPLOYEES

Employees tended to give the church higher marks for recruiting and hiring Blacks (37%) than administrators (26%). The same was true for the hiring of persons with disabilities; 30% of employees rated the church "excellent" to "good" whereas only 19% of the administrators did so. With the other affirmative action issues related to hiring and promoting the differences were slightly less than ten percentage points. Employees differed only on the promotion of women with male employees (64%) rating the church's efforts higher than female (54%) employees.

Education

Post graduate degrees were possessed by 71% of the male and 46% of the female employees. One fifth of both groups were high school graduates. However 34% of female employees were classified as "non-college graduates."

The education level of employees had an *inverse* effect only on the hiring of Blacks and persons with disabilities; the higher the education level the lower the rating given. The education level of employees had no significant effect on all other aspects of affirmative action being considered here.

Level of Satisfaction

According to the three "level of satisfaction" statements, 52% percent of employees were "very satisfied" to "somewhat satisfied." Male employees were somewhat more satisfied (55%) than female employees

Figure 3
Percent of Difference between Female Administrators and Male Administrators on Scale of Dissatisfaction

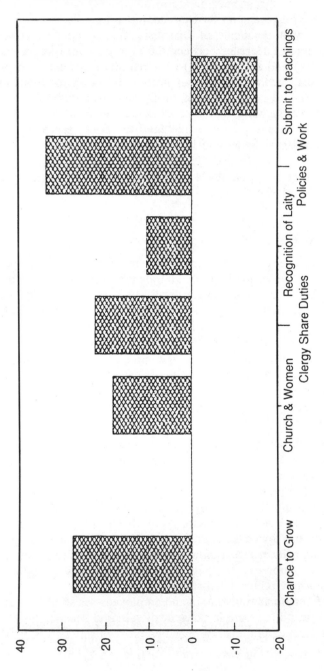

(50%).[6] Less than half of the female employees were "very satisfied" with their involvement in ministry and the recognition they receive. It should be noted that only one third of the males (37%) were "very satisfied" with the recognition they receive.

The level of employee satisfaction had a *direct* effect on how they evaluated the church's affirmative action position on the recruitment, hiring and promotion of all levels of minorities under consideration. The higher the level of education for employees the better the chance they would score the church's efforts "excellent" to "good."

TABLE 2
Level of Satisfaction Statements and Scores for Employees

	Percent Very Satisfied	
Satisfaction Statements	Male	Female
My involvement with ministry	57%	48%
The responsibility I have been given	70%	60%
The recognition I receive from my work	37%	41%
Average	55%	50%

Scale of Dissatisfaction

Employees were slightly less dissatisfied than were the administrators. Among employees 36% "completely agreed" or "agreed" with the dissatisfaction statements, whereas 41% of the administrators were in agreement. The average scores indicated that there was little difference between male (35%) and female (38%) employees.

Those who placed high with this scale had an *inverse* effect on the evaluations of the church's position on all aspects of recruitment, hiring, and promotion for women, Blacks, other minorities, persons with disabilities, young people, and people over 50 years.

PRESENT REALITY FOR AFFIRMATIVE ACTION IN THE CHURCH

The wide variations noted regarding the evaluation of hiring and promoting of minorities above ought to be confusing. Is the major issue one of "no policies"; or "policy but no programs"; or "policy with programs but few minorities hired"?

Are some administrators and employees satisfied because **affirmative action policies** are in place or dissatisfied because there are none?

Are some administrators and employees satisfied because **affirmative action programs** are functioning or dissatisfied because they are not?

Are some administrators and employees satisfied because they have a few minorities hired or dissatisfied because too few have been hired?

It would be useful to probe some facts.

Black, Hispanic, and Other Minorities Employed

In 1989 40 arch/diocesan offices, employing over 3,000 persons, employed 416 minorities as administrators or employees—1.4% of the total employed. (NCCIJ, 1989) Minority administrators numbered 126, employees totaled 290. Among these 40 arch/dioceses, 5 employed just over 50%, or 211 persons with 55 in administrative positions. The remaining 35 arch/dioceses employed but 205 minorities. These 35 arch/dioceses shared 71 minority administrators and 134 minority employees.

Blacks comprised 40% of the total employed and 39% of minority administrators. Hispanics were 47% of the total employed and 48% of minority administrators. Other minorities (Asian and Native American) accounted for the remainder.

Of the 416 minorities, administrators accounted for 30% of the total number employed; among the administrators males accounted for 54% and females 46%. Female employees accounted for 56% of the total.

Implications

The church is not employing Blacks and Hispanic minorities in any significant numbers. Whatever the reasons, the above data helps to explain some of the dissatisfaction noted earlier.

Possible Reasons Why Minority Employment is Low

When asked why more minorities were not employed some arch/dioceses noted:

Minorities do not apply
Salaries are too low to compete
Not many minorities reside nearby
A hiring "freeze" is in effect
The wrong approach was made in recruitment
No efforts had been made to recruit minorities

The reasons sound all too familiar for dioceses with affirmative action policies and some form of affirmative action programs.

The issue that now remains is to test the validity of the reasons.

A Potential Solution

The informal survey conducted by the National Catholic Conference for Interracial Justice (NCCIJ) was provocative because the respondents were all member dioceses with an office set up to promote minority hiring. The arch/bishops were presumably interested; but good will did not accomplish a great deal in the area of recruitment, hiring and promotion. More is required.

In a detailed analysis of two large dioceses a professional firm noted the weaknesses in the existing affirmative action programs, one dating from June 1980 and the other from May 1982. (These two dioceses are considered by the NCCIJ to have the best affirmative action programs in the States.) In each case no one person was really responsible for the implementation of the program. No reasonable method existed for tracking minority employees; no annual goals were set with department heads. No affirmative action training programs existed for current administrators and employees, nor did adequate training programs exist for minorities once they were hired. Numerous deficiencies were noted in the personnel policies, practices and procedures manuals. (NCCIJ, 1990)

The firm noted in closing one report: "There needs to be an expansion of (the 1980) commitment by developing a formal program with specific accountability for success and on-going auditing of results."

CHALLENGES

1. Policies and Practice for Blacks, Hispanics, and Others

The reasons given to the NCCIJ survey why racial and ethnic minorities were not being hired need to be carefully examined by each arch/diocese if the Catholic Church is to take its place with the more enlightened corporations and organizations in the United States. It is striking to find that two dioceses with policies for affirmative action were lacking in the implementation of those policies: lack of someone in charge, of clear objectives, and of a personnel tracking system.

The NCCIJ is currently developing training programs on affirmative action for use in four dioceses. Use is being made of the experience gained in government and the private sector. This program is based on the assumptions that "the diocese should practice what it proposes" to parishes and church institutions.

Administrators must respond to the growing demands of this multicultural church. Little is being done to improve on the employment of minorities and Blacks, other than women, in their hiring and promotion. The NACPA survey indicates this need, especially when compared with the NCCIJ informal survey which suggests that very little is actually being done.

2. Policies and Practices for Women, Young & Older Persons, and Persons with Disabilities

The church's record for hiring women received good marks. (About one-half of the administrators surveyed were women.) However, the Dissatisfaction Scale indicated clearly that at least one of every two female administrators is dissatisfied with some major aspect of employment. While the specific areas of dissatisfaction are beyond the scope of "affirmative action"' those areas definitely need further attention and study.

The practices for young and older persons need attention as less than half of the administrators gave the church "excellent" to "good" ratings for hiring young people. However, two-thirds felt the church has done well in hiring persons over age 50. Low marks were given for the employment practices regarding persons with disabilities.

CONCLUSION

This survey of church administrators and employees has raised many personnel issues which need to be clarified very quickly. Some of the affirmative action issues are clearly serious and portend deepening problems in the immediate future. For twenty-five years dioceses have been expanding staff in an attempt to provide assistance and guidance to parishes, schools, and the laity. If each diocese will not be able to recruit and retain competent personnel, and personnel representative of the multicultural church membership, then no one can expect that the Catholic Church in the United States will be able to respond to the growing needs of the educated laity and especially of women and the multicultural minorities.

FOOTNOTES

1. *Level of Education:* The Gallup Survey analyzed three levels: non-college graduate, college graduate, and post-graduate degree.

2. *Level of Satisfaction:* Factor analysis showed that three questions relating to satisfaction were very important: How satisfied are you with each of the following:

10a) My involvement in ministry (Very . . . Not At All)
10b) The responsibility I have been given (Very . . . Not At All)
10c) The recognition I receive for my work (Very . . . Not At All)

3. *Scale of Dissatisfaction:* Factor analysis indicated that the response to the following statements were very important.

6d) Many workers have become discouraged because the restrictive rules of the Church deny them the opportunity to grow and work in its service to their full ability. (Agree . . . Disagree)

11c) Many parishioners see no point in becoming involved with the Church because they object to its stand on issues such as the treatment of women. (Agree . . . Disagree)

11e) The clergy are reluctant to share their duties with sisters, brothers, lay workers, and ministers. (Agree . . . Disagree)

11f) Lay workers do not get enough recognition for their commitment and works. (Agree . . . Disagree)

14d) Unless the Church become more open in some of its policies, there may come a time when I can no longer continue working for the Church. (Very True . . . Not At All True)

14e) No matter how much I disagree, I must always submit to the will and the teachings of the Church. (Very True . . . Not At All True)

4. *Level of Satisfaction:* The average for all administrators is useful in the text as there is less than ten percentage points separation; the same is true for male and female scores. All scores indicated the percent "very satisfied":

	Male	Female	Difference
10a) My involvement in Ministry			
	64.8%	55.1%	-9.7%
10b) Responsibility I have been given			
	72.6%	64.2%	-8.4%
10c) The recognition I receive			
	46.1%	46.7%	+0.6%
Average	61.2%	55.3%	-5.9%

5. **Scale of Dissatisfaction:** The average is used for convenience. Since the female average is 15 percentage points higher it is useful to indicate where the differences occur and the magnitude: Administrators

	Male	Female	Difference
6d) Church denies opportunity to grow			
	30.5%	58.0%	+27.5%
11c) Church's treatment of women			
	11.4%	29.6%	+ 18.2%
11e) Clergy reluctant to share duties			
	31.2%	53.6%	+22.4%
11f) Laity don't get enough recognition			
	59.4%	69.8%	+10.4%
14d) Policies may cause me to cease work			
	23.8%	57.3%	+37.5%
14e) I must always submit to teachings			
	44.0%	28.6%	-15.4%
Average	36.8	51.9	+15.1%

6. *Level of Satisfaction*: The average for all employees is useful in the text as there is less than ten percentage points separation; the same is true for male and female scores. All scores indicated the percent "very satisfied":

	Male	Female	Difference
10a) My involvement in Ministry			
	56.6%	47.7%	-8.9%
10b) Responsibility I have been given			
	69.9%	59.6%	-10.3%
10c) The recognition I receive			
	37.1%	41.1%	+4.0%
Average	64.5%	49. 5%	-5.0%

Contributors

COLLEEN BRANAGAN, MS, is the Director for Lay Personnel for the Archdiocese of Seattle. Colleen has co-authored *Diocesan Lay Retirement Systems* and *Just Treatment for Those Who Work for the Church*, NACPA publications, and has presented workshops on personnel issues. She has a master's degree in Human Resource Management.

WILLIAM P. DALY, MS, is the Director of Consultation Services for the National Association of Church Personnel Administrators. Bill has served in personnel administration at Oberlin College in Ohio, at California State University in Los Angeles, and as a personnel analyst for the California Department of Transportation. Bill holds a Master of Science degree in public administration.

MARY ELLEN McCLANAGHAN, PhD, is an Assistant Professor of Religious Studies and Chair of the Division of Letters at Marygrove College, Detroit, MI. Mary Ellen is a trained group facilitator and consultant. Her areas of expertise include adult education, human resource management, and educational design and evaluation. Mary Ellen has a doctorate in instructional technology.

LUCIEN ROY, STL, is the Director of the Office for Ministry Formation for the Archdiocese of Chicago. Lucien is a consultant, facilitator, and speaker in areas of ministry formation and organizational development. Lucien has graduate degrees in philosophy and theology and has pursued doctoral studies in the history of theology.

REV. FRANCIS KELLY SHEETS, OSC, PhD, is a member of the Crozier Fathers and Brothers province and Director of Planning for Church Management, Planning and Management Information. He has directed strategic planning studies for parishes, schools, dioceses, and religious congregations for over ten years. He formerly served as coordinator of Church Management Programs for the Center for Applied Research in the Apostolate. He holds a doctorate in philosophy.

ANN MARIE WINTERS, JCL, is a canon lawyer and parish consultant in conflict resolution. She is the director of Cincinnati Mediation Services which provides services in conflict management and resolution for churches and divorce and family mediation for individuals. Ann Marie has served as judge and assistant director of the Marriage Tribunal in the archdiocese of Cincinnati. She holds a licentiate degree in Canon Law.

PATRICIA WITTBERG, SC, is on the faculty of Indiana University, Indianapolis, IN, and was formerly Assistant Professor of Sociology at Fordham University in New York City. She holds a doctorate in sociology from the University of Chicago. Patricia has published several articles on sociology of religion and religious organizations as well as urban sociology. She published a book on patterns of organization in religious congregations, *Creating a Future for Religious Life*.

Bibliography

PART I: SOCIOLOGICAL ANALYSIS

Ammerman, Nancy T. (1990). *Baptist Battles.* New Brunswick: Rutgers University Press.

Archdiocese of Indianapolis. (1984). "Report of the Urban Ministry Study." Archdiocese of Indianapolis, IN.

Bernstein, Paul. (1976). *Workplace Democratization: Its Internal Dynamics.* Kent, OH: Kent State University Press.

Blau, Peter. (1973). Dynamics of Bureaucracy. 2nd edition. Chicago: University of Chicago Press.

Bolick, Clint and Susan Nestleroth. (1988). *Opportunity 2000: Creative Affirmative Action Strategies for a Changing Workforce.* U.S. Department of Labor.

Branagan, Colleen T. (1990, February). "Diocesan and Parish Collaboration in Developing Parish Personnel Systems." *Church Personnel Issues.* Cincinnati, OH: National Association of Church Personnel Administrators.

Braverman, Harry. (1974). *Labor and Monopoly Capitalism: The Degradation of Work in the Twentieth Century.* NY, NY: Monthly Review Press.

"Catholic Church Personnel in the U.S.: A Report of the Task Force." (1984).

Collins, Randall. (1979). *The Credential Society.* New York: Academic Press.

Conscience. (1988). "All Work and No Say." *Conscience* 9:6.

Coy, William J. (1988, November). "Contracts: Worth the Paper?" *Church Personnel Issues.* Cincinnati, OH: National Assocation of Church Personnel Administrators.

Crozier, Michel. (1964). *The Bureaucratic Phenomenon.* Chicago: University of Chicago Press.

Dahm, Charles W. (1981). *Power and Authority in the Catholic Church: Cardinal Cody in Chicago.* Notre Dame, IN: University of Notre Dame Press.

Davis, Kingsley, and Wilbert Moore. (1945). "Some Principles of Stratification." *American Sociological Review* 10:242-249.

Dolan, Jay P., editor. (1987). *The American Catholic Parish: A History From 1850 to the Present.* New York: Paulist.

Dudley, Roger. (1990, November). "The Status of Female Leadership in the Seventh Day Adventist Church as Perceived by Women Leaders." Paper read at the conference of the Society for the Scientific Study of Religion, Virginia Beach.

Fallows, James. (1984, December). "The Case Against Credentialism." *Atlantic Monthly*, pp. 49-67.

Fein, Mitchell. (1976). "Motivation for Work." in Robert Dubin, editor, *Handbook of Work. Organization and Society.* Chicago: Rand McNally, pp. 465-530.

Ference, Thomas P. et. al. (1971). "Priests and Church: The Professionalization of an Organization." *American Behavioral Scientist* 14:507-524.

Fichter, Joseph. (1988). *A Sociologist Looks at Religion.* Wilmington, DE: Michael Glazier.

Fogarty, John C. (1988). *The Catholic Priest: His Identity and Values.* Kansas City: Sheed & Ward.

Fox, Zenobia. (1986). "A Post-Vatican II Phenomenon: Lay Ministries." PhD Dissertation, Fordham University.

Galle, Omer R. et al. (1985). "Racial Mix and Industrial Productivity." *American Sociological Review* 50:20-33.

Garson, Barbara. (1988). *The Electronic Sweatshop.* New York: Penguin Books.

Giniat, Irene, (In process). "Sisters Councils in the U.S." PhD Dissertation, University of Wisconsin.

Glenn, Evelyn and Rosalyn Feldberg. (1977). "Degraded and Deskilled: The Proletarianization of Clerical Work." *Social Problems* 25:5264.

Goldner, Fred, et al. (1977). "The Production of Cynical Knowledge in Organizations." *American Sociological Review* 42:539-551.

Granovetter, Marc. (1977). "The Strength of Weak Ties." *American Journal of Sociology* 78:13-61.

Greeley, Andrew. (1977). (a) *The Catholic Priest in the U.S.: A Sociological Investigation.* Washington, DC: United States Catholic Conference. (b) *Priests in the U.S.* (1972) New York: Doubleday.

Greeley, Andrew and William McManus. (1987). *Catholic Contributions: Sociology and Policy.* Chicago: Thomas More Press.

Gutierriz-Johnson, Anna and William Foote Whyte. (1976, September). "The Mondragon System of Worker Production Cooperatives." *Social Experience.*

Hall, Douglas T. and Benjamin Schneider. (1973). *Organizational Climates and Careers: The Work Lives of Priests.* New York: Seminar Press.

Harrison, Paul. (1959). *Authority and Power in the Free Church Tradition.* Princeton, NJ: Princeton University Press.

Hay Group. "Linking New Employee Attitudes and Values to Improving Productivity, Cost and Quality." Research for Management Report.

Herzberg, Frederick. (a) (1966). *Work and the Nature of Man.* New York: Crowell.(b) (1982) Managerial Choice: *To be Efficient and to be Human.* New York: Olympia.

Heslin, Julia A. (1983). "In Transition: A Study of Women Religious Administrators in Nontraditional Roles." PhD Dissertation. Fordham University.

Hirschmann. A. 0. (1970). *Exit. Voice and Loyalty.* Cambridge, MA: Harvard University Press.

Hodson, Randy and Teresa Sullivan. (1990). *The Social Organization of Work.* Belmont, CA: Wadsworth Publishers.

Hoge, Dean R. (1987). *The Future of Catholic Leadership.* Kansas City: Sheed & Ward.

Hoge, Dean R., Jackson Carroll and Francis K. Scheets. (1988). *Patterns of Parish Leadership.* Kansas City: Sheed & Ward.

Hoge, Dean R. et al. (a) (1988). "Changing Age Distributions and the Theological Attitudes of Catholic Priests: 1970-1985." *Sociological Analysis* 49:264-280. (b) (1983). "Research on Men's Vocations to the Priesthood and Religious Life." Washington, DC: National Conference of Catholic Bishops.

House, Robert J. and Lawrence A. Wigdor. (1967). "Herzberg's DualFactor Theory of Job Satisfaction and Motivation: A Review of the Evidence and a Criticism." *Personnel Psychology* 20: 369-389.

Hunnius, Gerry et al. (1973). *Workers' Control: A Reader on Labor and Social Change.* New York: Random House.

Ingram, Larry. (1980). "Notes on Pastoral Power in the Congregational Tradition." *Journal for the Scientific Study of Religion* 19:4048.

Joseph, S. M. Vincentia et al. (1982). "New Ministries of Women Religious: Role Conflict and Coping Styles." Washington, DC: Religious Formation Conference.

Kanter, Rosabeth M. (1977). *Men and Women of the Corporation.* New York: Basic Books.

Kantowicz, Edward R. (a) (1983). *Corporation Sole: Cardinal Mundelein and Chicago Catholicism.* Notre Dame, IN: University of

Notre Dame Press. (b) (1980). "Church and Neighborhood." Ethnicity 7:349-366.

Kelly, Maryellen and Bennett Harrison. (1990, August 13). "Innovations in LaborManagement Problem Solving." Paper read at the American Sociological Association's Annual Convention, Washington, DC.

Kim, Gertrud, OSB. (1980). "Roman Catholic Organization Since Vatican II." In Ross P. Scherer, et al. *American Denominational Organization*. Pasadena, CA: William Carey.

Kinsella, Larkin, J. (1989) (a) "Survey of the NACPA Membership." Cincinnati, OH: National Association of Church Personnel Administrators. (b) (1989) "State of Personnel in Largest Parishes of U.S. Dioceses." Cincinnati, OH: National Association of Church Personnel Administrators.

LaMagdeleine, Donald R. (1986). "U.S. Catholic Church Related Jobs as Dual Labor Markets: A Speculative Inquiry." *Review for Religious Research* 27:315-327.

McManus, Jim. (1987, August 27). "Boston Lobstermen's Coop Has Archdiocese Backing." *National Catholic Reporter*, p. 11.

McPherson and SmithLovin. (1984). "Women and Weak Ties." *American Journal of Sociology* 87:883-904.

Meyer, John W. and Brian Rowan. (1980). "Institutionalized Organizations: Formal Structure as Myth and Ceremony." In Amitai Etzioni and Edward Lehman, editors. *A Sociological Reader in Complex Organizations*, Second edition. New York: Holt, pp. 300-318.

Michels, Robert. (1984). "Oligarchy." In Frank Fischer and Carmen Sirianni, editors. *Critical Studies in Organization and Bureaucracy*. Philadelphia: Temple University Press, pp. 48-64.

National Organization for the Continuing Education of Roman Catholic Clergy. (1986). "Basic Information for the Continued Formation of Clergy." *Resource* 13.

National Conference of Catholic Bishops. (1982). (a) "Parish Life in the U.S. (Notre Dame Study) (1984) (b) "The Continuing Formation of Priests: Growing in Wisdom, Age and Grace."

Neal, Marie Augusta. (1984). *Catholic Sisters in Transition*. Wilmington, DE: Michael Glazier.

Neff, Walter S. (1985). *Work and Human Behavior*, Third edition. New York: Aldine.

O'Brien, David J. (1989, November) "Justice in the Church: Historical Perspectives." *Church Personnel Issues*. Cincinnati, OH: National Association of Church Personnel Administrators.

Ouchi, William. (1982). *Theory Z: How American Business Can Meet the Japanese Challenge*. New York: Avon Books.

Pavalko, Roland M. (1988). *Sociology of Occupations and Professions*, Second edition. Itasca, IL: Peacock Publishers.

Perrow, Charles. (1986). *Complex Organizations: A Critical Essay*, Second edition. New York: Random House.

Peterson, Robert A. and Richard Schoenherr. (1978). "Organizational Status Attainment of Religious Professionals." *Social Forces* 56:794-822.

Pfeiffer, Jeffrey. (1980). *Power in Organizations.* Marshfield, MA: Pittman.

Pugh, Derek S. and David J. Hickson. (1989). *Writers of Organizations*, Fourth edition. Newbury Park, CA: Sage Publications.

Reese, Thomas J. (1989). *Archbishop: Inside the Power Structure of the American Catholic Church.* New York: Harper & Row.

Rosenberg, Florence and Edward M. Sullivan. (1980). *Women and Ministry: A Survey of the Experience of Roman Catholic Women in the U.S.* Washington, DC: Center for Applied Research in the Apostolate.

Salaman, Graeme. (1981). *Work Organization and Class Structure.* New York: M. E. Sharpe.

Sandoval, Moises. (1990). *On the Move: A History of the Hispanic Church in the U.S.* Maryknoll, NY: Orbis Books.

Scheets, Francis K., OSC (a) (1989) "The Challenge of Change: A Collaborative Parish Ministry." Church Personnel Issues. Cincinnati, OH: National Association of Church Personnel Administrators (b) "Clergy Survey of Elizabeth, New Jersey."

Schoenherr, Richard A. and Andrew Greeley. (1974). "Role Commitment Processes and the American Catholic Priesthood." *American Sociological Review* 39:407-426.

Schoenherr, Richard A. and Annemette Sorenson. (1982). "Social Change in Religious Organizations: Consequences of Clergy Decline in the U.S. Catholic Church." *Sociological Analysis* 43:23-52.

Schoenherr, Richard A. et al. (1988). "Demographic Transition in Religious Organizations: A Comparative Study of Priest Decline in Roman Catholic Dioceses." *Journal for the Scientific Study of Religion* 27:499-523.

Shaiken, Harley. (1986). *Work Transformed: Automation and Labor in the Computer Age.* Lexington, MA: Lexington Books.

Struzzo, John A. (1970). "Professionalism and the Resolution of Authority Conflicts Among the Catholic Clergy." *Sociological Analysis* 31:92-106.

Szafran, Robert F. (a) (1980) "Ethnicity and Status Attainment: The Case of Roman Catholic Clergy." *Sociological Quarterly* 21:41-51.

"Ten Years Later, The Glass Ceiling Gleams." (1990, Sept. 3) *Newsweek*, p. 52.

Vera, Hernan. (1982) *Professionalization and Professionalism of Catholic Priests.* Gainesville, FL: University of Florida Press.

Weber, Max. (1984). "Bureaucracy." In Frank Fischer and Carmen Sirianni, editors. *Critical Studies in Organization and Bureaucracy.* Philadelphia: Temple University Press.

Wittberg, Patricia (a) (1989). "The Dual Labor Market in the Catholic Church." *Review for Religious Research* 30:287-290. (b) (1989) "Nonordained Workers in the Catholic Church." *Journal for the Scientific Study of Religion* 28:148-161. (c) (1989). "Feminist Consciousness Among American Nuns: Patterns of Ideological Diffusion." *Women's Studies International Forum* 12:5, 529-537.

Zwerdling, Daniel. (1984). *Workplace Democracy.* New York: Harper & Row.

PART II: REFLECTIONS ON THE SOCIOLOGICAL ANALYSIS

Training and Development

Best, F. (1985, January). "The Nature of Work in a Changing Society." *Personnel Journal,* pp. 37-42.

Carnevale, A., Gainer, L and Villet, J. (1990). *Training in America: The Organization and Strategic Role of Training.* San Francisco: Jossey- Bass, Inc. Publishers.

Caudron, S. and Rozek, M. (1990, July). "The Wellness Payoff." *Personnel Journal,* pp. 54-62.

Coates, J., Jarratt, J. and Mahaffie, J. (1990). *Future Work: Seven Critical Forces Reshaping Work and the Work Force in North America.* San Francisco:Jossey-Bass, Inc. Publishers.

Conscience. (1988). "All Work and No Say." 9 (6).

Costello, T. (1987, June). "Connections of the Just Treatment Paper With the Bishop's Pastoral on the Economy." (Available from NACPA, 100 East Eighth St., Cincinnati, Ohio, 45202).

Fogarty, J. (1988). *The Catholic Priest: His Identity and Values.* Kansas City: Sheed & Ward.

Johnston, W. and Packer, A. (1990). *Workforce 2000: Work and Workers for the 21st Century.* Indianapolis: Hudson Institute.

Kiley, J.C. (1987, June). "Church Personnel Today." (Available from NACPA, 100 East Eighth St., Cincinnati, Ohio, 45202).

La Magdeleine, D. (1986). *U.S. Catholic Church Related Jobs as Dual Labor Markets.* 27 (4).

Nadler, L and Nadler, Z. (1989). *Developing Human Resources.* San Francisco: Jossey-Bass Publishers.

Naisbitt, J. and Aburdene, P. (1990). *Megatrends 2000: Ten New Directions for the 1990's.* New York: William Morrow and Company, Inc.

National Association of Church Personnel Administrators. (1986, November). *Just Treatment for Those Who Work for the Church.* (Available from NACPA, 100 East Eighth St., Cincinnati, Ohio, 45202).

Posner, B. and Schmidt, W. (1988, Spring) "Government Morale and Management: A Survey of Federal Executives." *Public Personnel Management* 17(1). pp 21-27.

Sutcliffe, J and Schuster, J. (1985, September) "Benefits Revisited, Benefits Predicted." *Personnel Journal.* pp 62-68.

Taylor, H. (1986, April) "Power at Work." *Personnel Journal,* pp 42-49.

Recruitment, Retention, Job Descriptions, Performance Appraisals

Just Treatment for Those Who Work for the Church, (1986). National Association of Church Personnel Administrators. (Available from NACPA, 100 East 8th Street, Cincinnati, Ohio 45202.)

Coordinating Parish Ministries, (1987). Department of Personnel Services, Archdiocese of Chicago. (Available from Chicago Catholic Publications, 1144 West Jackson Boulevard, Chicago, Illinois 60611.)

Pathfinder for Compensation Systems: A NACPA Working Paper, (1989). National Association of Church Personnel Administrators. (Available from NACPA, 100 East 8th Street, Cincinnati, Ohio 45202.)

Employment Grievances

Ewing, David W. *Justice on the Job.* Boston: Harvard Business School Press, 1989.

Just Treatment For Those Who Work for the Church, (1986). Cincinnati: National Association of Church Personnel Administrators, 1986.

Kennedy, Robert T. s.v. "Due Process." *New Catholic Encyclopedia* 16:135

Provost, James, ed. *Due Process in the United States: Report on a Task Force Survey,* (1985). Washington, D.C.: Canon Law Society of America.

Rowe, Mary and Baker, Michael. (1984, May-June) "Are You Hearing Enough Employee Concerns?" *Harvard Business Review,* pp. 127-135.

Compensation

Milkovich, George T. & Newman, Jerry M., (1990). *Compensation.* Richard C. Irwin, Inc.

Just Treatment for Those Who Work for the Church, (1986, November). National Association of Church Personnel Administrators. (Available from NACPA, 100 E. 8th St., Cincinnati, Ohio 45202.)

Diocesan Lay Retirement Systems: Current Status and Future Directions, (1988). National Association of Church Personnel Administrators. (Available from NACPA, 100 E. 8th St., Cincinnati, Ohio 45202.)

Just Wages and Benefits for Lay and Religious Church Employees, (1990). National Catholic Conference of Diocesan Directors of Religious Education. (Available from NCDD, 3021 4th St., N.E., Washington, D.C. 20017.)

Affirmative Action

Conscience (Nov./Dec. 1988). "All Work and No Say"

Just Treatment for Those Who Work for the Church, (1986). NACPA (Available from NACPA, 100 E. 8th St., Cincinnati, OH 45202).

La Magdeleine, Donald R. (1986). "U.S. Catholic Church-Related Jobs as Dual Labor Markets: A Speculative Inquiry." *Review for Religious Research*.

National Catholic Conference for Interracial Justice (NCCIJ), (1989). Affirmative Action in US Catholic *Dioceses: An Informal Telephone Survey Report by NCCIJ*, 11 pages. A telephone survey with previously assigned and informed diocesan coordinators. Eleven archdioceses and 29 dioceses participated, representing 30% of total Catholic population. Catholic Charities personnel were not included in this survey. The data used in the current section was obtained from this internal document.

NCCIJ (1990). *Affirmative Action Analysis of the...Central Office* by Walker & Walker, Inc.; confidential documents.

Rosenberg, Florence R., and Sullivan, Edward M. (1980). *Women and Ministry: A Survey of the Experience of Roman Catholic Women in the United States*. Washington: Center for Applied Research in the Apostolate.